AVERAGE JOE

AVERAGE JOE

The Memoirs of a
Blue-Collar Entertainer

JOE PISCOPO

Forefront
BOOKS

Published by Forefront Books, Nashville, Tennessee.
Distributed by Simon & Schuster.

Library of Congress Control Number: 2024922274

Print ISBN: 978-1-63763-356-4
E-book ISBN: 978-1-63763-357-1

Cover Design by Bruce Gore, Gore Studio, Inc.
Interior Design by Interior Design by PerfecType, Nashville, TN
Printed in the United States of America

DEDICATION &
ACKNOWLEDGMENTS

I dedicate this book to my dear family.

With infinite and loving gratitude to my dear parents, Edith Ida and Joseph P. Piscopo.

- Heartfelt love with great pride to my beautiful children, Joey, Alexandra, Michael, Olivia, and Charley. And to their moms for blessing me with the best kids in the world.

And to you—I am always humbled by the goodness and kindness of everyday folks.

And last but not least, sincere respect and appreciation to my mentor and friend, Raymond Mirra.

TABLE OF CONTENTS

Prologue: Where's Eddie?   9

Part 1
FROM AVELLINO TO NEW JERSEY

1. Coming to America   15
2. Jersey Boy   27
3. American Pastoral   41
4. Jonesing & Catatonia Dreaming   59

Part 2
IF YOU CAN MAKE IT THERE,
YOU'LL MAKE IT ANYWHERE

5. A Stand-Up Guy   69
6. With a Little Help from My Friends   87
7. Commercial Breaks & Breaking In   97

Part 3
LIVE FROM NEW YORK,
IT'S SATURDAY NIGHT!

8. The Jersey Guy Auditions at 30 Rock   105
9. I've Got the World on a String: *SNL* Season 6 | 1980–1981   113
10. It's ~~Not~~ a Tumor   123
11. Eddie   129
12. Crazy, Man. Crazy: *SNL* Season 7 | 1981–1982   135

13. One Toke over the Cocaine Line   145
14. Mr. Sinatra   153
15. Under Pressure: *SNL* Season 8 | 1982–1983   163
16. Merry Old Souls: *SNL* Season 9 | 1983–1984   167
17. Exiting Dick Ebersol's *SNL*   177

Part 4
JAMMIN' ME

18. Dork Dad & Divorce   185
19. Hollywood Hits & Almost Theres   189
20. An Evening at the White House   207
21. Muscles & Critics   211

Part 5
WHERE HAVE YOU GONE, JOE PISCOPO?

22. Lean on Me: Helping Newark's Neediest   219
23. Dork Dad & Divorce II   225
24. That's Life   233

Postscript: Me & Mr. Trump   243
Endnotes   247

WHERE'S EDDIE?

It's 11:20 p.m. in New York City. At the studios of NBC-TV—30 Rock—*Saturday Night Live* is minutes away from yet another live broadcast in Studio 8H.

And they can't find Eddie Murphy.

Producers, stage managers, and production assistants scramble in a panic.

"Where's Eddie?" someone asks.

"We're almost on! Gotta find Eddie," another fellow shouts.

"Get Piscopo!" says a third. "Get Piscopo to get Eddie."

I always knew my role on *SNL*. The utility guy. If they needed something no one else could do . . . or, more likely, didn't want to do, "Get Piscopo. He'll do it."

I'm hustling out of the makeup room to get myself set in the studio for our cold open.

The barrage of panicked folks hit me hard. "Joe, you've gotta find Eddie!"

We're live at 11:30, and it is now 11:22.

This being a weekly ritual, I know exactly where Eddie is.

And being a good soldier, I tell everyone not to worry, I'll be right back. With Eddie.

A good soldier indeed. But a better friend. I don't want to spill the beans on my buddy.

So I slip away to where I know Eddie will be—the offices of *SNL* on the seventeenth floor.

You have to take two elevators to get there. Legend has it that Lorne Michaels, our Grand High Exalted Mystic Ruler and the genius creator of *Saturday Night Live*, did not want studio executives near John Belushi. And vice versa. So Lorne created a bit of a firewall with the elevators.

The offices are dead quiet, unlike each weekday when we frantically scramble for material for that week's show.

———

I finally reach Eddie's office. The door is closed, and I know exactly what is going on.

I have never seen anyone so smooth and successful with a woman. The guy is an absolute magnet.

I politely yet forcefully knock on the door and say, "Eddie, it's time."

Through the door, Eddie says, "I got it. I'm on my way."

I said, "Eddie, let's do this. Showtime!"

———

One of my fondest memories is of Eddie and me bursting out of the elevator doors and flying down the eighth-floor hallway.

We hear stage manager Joe Dicso inside the studio yelling, "Ten seconds to air!"

The studio doors are held open by all of those concerned folks who were looking for Eddie earlier.

Dicso's purposely forced, frantic call of "Five seconds!" draws a big laugh from the studio audience.

Eddie and I step in front of the cameras as the *SNL* band kicks in and Don Pardo makes his legendary announcement, "It's *Saturday Night Live!*"

Eddie is in the house.

Part 1

FROM AVELLINO TO NEW JERSEY

Family Roots

COMING TO AMERICA

A nyone who loves peanut butter and jelly sandwiches can tell you that "With a name like Smuckers, it has to be good." That simple tagline sprang from the mind of an ad agency copywriter as she pondered how to use the fun and distinct last name of the jelly maker's founder.

None of us has any say about the family we're born into or the name we inherit. But I've always felt like I was blessed by God because, with a family name like Piscopo, it has to be Italian. And as I see it, being born into my family means I won the lottery of birth.

As an Italian American, I find immense pride in the rich tapestry of my heritage. My roots trace back to a land renowned for its history, culture, and contributions to civilization. Italians made significant contributions throughout history, from the Renaissance artists like Leonardo da Vinci, Galileo Galilei, and Michelangelo, who shaped the world of art and science, to modern-day technology heroes like Guglielmo Marconi, Alessandro Volta, and Enrico Fermi. With all

15

due respect to Alexander Graham Bell, it was the Italian American Antonio Meucci who first invented the telephone.[1]

And I haven't even mentioned all the Italian-inspired culinary traditions that have become staples in American households. Pizza anyone?

"In 1492," Italian explorer Christopher Columbus "sailed the ocean blue" looking for Asia and instead found the New World when he landed in . . . the Bahamas? Another great Italian explorer followed Columbus and wound up giving his first name to the continents: Amerigo Vespucci. Italians have been coming to the Americas—and to the United States—ever since.

It was the journey of almost five million Italians who emigrated to the US in a great wave during the late nineteenth and early twentieth centuries that testifies to their resilience and determination. They faced great challenges and discrimination yet carved out a space for themselves and contributed to the cultural fabric of America.

The legacy of Italian Americans is evident in sports, politics, and the arts. Baseball icons like Joe DiMaggio and Yogi Berra played some of the greatest baseball ever, and legendary football coach Vince Lombardi is the namesake of the Super Bowl trophy.

In politics, revered Italian Americans include the great New York Mayor Fiorello La Guardia, Congressman Steve Scalise, and the late Supreme Court Justice Antonin Scalia.

From movie directors like Martin Scorsese and Francis Ford Coppola to actors like Al Pacino, Chazz Palminteri, and singers like my own hero, Frank Sinatra, our community has left an indelible mark on American culture.

And speaking of Coppola, it was he who teamed up with an aspiring Italian American novelist named Mario Puzo to produce what is widely regarded as one of the greatest films of all time: *The Godfather*.

I almost hate to bring up the film, because in light of all the massive contributions that real-life Italians have made to the world and to our country, why mention a fictitious story at all? My role models were the men and women in my family and the icons of the Italian American community, like those mentioned above—not fictional characters from a movie.

I'm sensitive to that and almost would strike out mentioning the *Godfather* films at all, except that in part 2 of the trilogy, there's that wonderful scene where the young boy escapes from Italy, crosses the ocean on a steamer, and lands on Ellis Island. Coppola filmed the kid standing on the ship's deck alongside hundreds of other immigrants, all gazing at the Statue of Liberty with a look of hope and wonder. Their clothes are frayed, and they have very few belongings—but they have American flags in their hand. It's a beautiful scene.

And here's where it gets personal for me. The steamship in that scene is extremely similar to a steamship that brought my own ancestors to America during that same period. I've got a picture of it on my wall, and I think of them every day. They passed through Ellis Island and went right to work building a new life in the new land of promise and freedom.

The novel and the film open with these lines, spoken by a mortician named Amerigo Bonasera:

"I believe in America. America has made my fortune."

I love those lines, and here's why: There's no better land to have come from than Italy, and there's no better nation to be a citizen of than America.

The name Amerigo Bonasera means something like "America, good night." Sounds ominous, right? Puzo wrote the novel from 1965 to 1968 and published it in 1969, the same four years I spent in high school in New Jersey. If you know anything at all about US history, then you know those years were full of upheaval and unrest, assassinations, the Vietnam War, protests, the battle for civil rights, and a widening gap between the generations. Fathers and sons watched the same nightly news but came to very different conclusions about what it all meant.

Would we Piscopos get torn apart by external pressures? Was the sun setting on America?

No! And my own life story—my family, upbringing, opportunities, blessings, friendships, and survival through the fire—testifies to that fact. Because of God, family, and this great nation we live in, the best is yet to be.

Avellino

In the fall of 2019, I led a group of American tourists through Italy on a trip sponsored by WNYM, the radio station where I do my daily show. The great folks at Perillo Tours surprised me with a side-trip over to my ancestral hometown of Pratola Serra in the province of Avellino. When we pulled up to the city hall with two busloads of American tourists, Mayor Emanuele Aufiero and town dignitaries welcomed me like I was the pope. With my picture up on the wall, they played Sinatra and gave me special recognition—in "the local boy who made good" style. They had arranged it so my relatives from Pratola Serra were there—some of whom I knew and some I met for the first time. I walked the same streets that my grandfather walked when he was a boy. And these were the same streets my father walked when he visited as a soldier in the US Army. I heard about relatives who had died fighting for Mussolini, involuntarily, during the Second World War—before the rest of Italy hung him up by his heels.

The stresses of abject poverty, political upheaval, and war all worked to rip the families apart. The Italians were resilient, though. I don't know how they did it, those earlier generations. I'm grateful they hung on—I owe them my life. Walking the streets of Pratola Serra with my kin was an experience that moved me like nothing else.

Mario Puzo was born in 1920 in Hell's Kitchen, New York City. My father was born in 1916 in Newark, New Jersey. Puzo's father emigrated to America from Pietradefusi, just five miles north of Pratola

Serra. That is to say, both Puzo and my father were first-generation Americans, with fathers who unknowingly had grown up within minutes of each other in the neighboring towns of Avellino. Our families' successes flowed from that singular decision by those "fortunate pilgrims" (as Puzo titled his first novel)—the brave men and women who decided to strike out and find a new life in this God-blessed country.

———————

The city of Avellino is also where the fictitious Tony Soprano's ancestry traces back to, prompting its real-life mayor initially to fear that the HBO series *The Sopranos* would tarnish the city's image. "I don't know why they had to pick us. We're not Corleone," Mayor Antonio di Nunno once complained.[2] It's important to note that the late actor James Gandolfini was loved and respected and one of the great Italian American talents of all time.

Antonio di Nunno? What a name. Reminds me of a sketch I did for my 1984 HBO special where I played the naive lead of a Jersey Boy-styled quartet called "The Deltones." We sang a special song I wrote for the guest of honor, who wound up being a mob boss (played by actor Anthony Caruso).

> *Tony DiNono.*
> *I can't believe that's your name.*
> *It seems such a shame.*
> *That Tony DiNono's your name.*
>
> *Tony, you are really where it's at.*
> *But that name has just got to go.*
> *Tony, who would give you a name like that?*
> *I don't know. You don't know. We don't know.*

At the end of the song, of course, we got whacked, rolled up into carpets, and thrown into the alley by the muscle.

I got the idea for the sketch from the night I unknowingly mocked a mafia hitman who was in the audience during my early days doing stand-up. I ended up with a broken nose and a trip to the ER, plus $10,000 in "go away" cash from a mob lawyer whom my dad talked to about how you can't just go around breaking comedians' noses. True story (see chapter 5).

————————

My maternal grandparents were Francesco and Speranza LaMagna. They emigrated from the city of Salerno, Italy, to New Jersey—first to Newark and then northward to Rutherford. My grandmother was so smart and financially astute that she eventually owned three homes off of Orient Way, which she used for income and investment. My grandparents had a mortgage on the three homes, and my grandmother would make her payments in cash every month. She would say, "I have to go pay the mortgage," and then she'd carry some olive oil with her to give to the banker.

Let me tell you how important that is and what an inspiration that is to me. Here they were, immigrants to the nation and happy to be here. The Italians were put down when they began arriving in large numbers. As they got off the boat, they weren't English-speaking Caucasians. They were suspect. But my grandparents had ten kids, bought three homes where family and renters could live, and got down to work becoming a successful part of their new country.

————————

I remember well my paternal grandparents, Rosario and Carmela (née Spiezio) Piscopo. Grandpa Rosario came to America aboard the SS *Moltke*, arriving at Ellis Island in 1907. I wish I could go back and ask my grandparents a million questions. Why did you leave your homeland? What were you thinking? What were your first thoughts when you arrived? Were you afraid? I asked my father everything—nothing left unsaid. But with my grandparents, I let time get away, and then they were gone. It was only afterward that I checked the records and archives at Ellis Island and discovered a lot about them.

Rosario and Carmela married and settled in the First Ward of Newark, also called the North Ward, which is today called the Seventh Avenue neighborhood. Italians first settled into the First Ward in the 1870s, crossing the Hudson River from New York City to look for work. In fact, the first twenty-seven Italian men in the First Ward had emigrated from Avellino. In 1873, these men found lodging on Boyden Street, just minutes from Mount Prospect Avenue, where my father would later be born and raised. This whole area of Newark became known as "Little Italy" and would come to mirror and even rival the Italian-populated sections of other major cities in America. By 1920, the Italians living in Newark numbered 27,465.[3]

Rosario and Carmela brought their second son—my dad—into the world and named him Pasquale Giuseppe Piscopo—but everyone called him Joe. Pop was raised on Mount Prospect Avenue, close to where it intersects with Bloomfield Avenue. My father always told me, "The crossroads of the world was at the intersection of Broad and Market Street in Newark." To my pop, that was it, man. It was Newark, New Jersey. And, like most immigrants in Newark, he always talked about "moving up Bloomfield Avenue"—because the further "up" you went, the less densely populated and more affluent the neighborhoods became. Extra Waspy. Better schools, parks, and less crime—that was the general idea.

Rosario worked in a hat factory located a block away from the radio station in lower Manhattan, where I now do my daily talk show. We're at 111 Broadway, and my grandfather worked at 185 Broadway and became quite good at what he did.

My pop had asthma when he was young, so my grandparents moved out to "the country," which back then meant Belleville, New Jersey, and my grandfather commuted to work. Belleville is known as the "Cherry Blossom Capital of America" because it has more cherry trees than even the famous Tidal Basin in the nation's capital. It really is a beautiful place.

They bought 511 Joralemon Street in Belleville—the house is still there today—and put Pop in Belleville Elementary School, right across the street. He couldn't speak English, though, so the class made fun of him. They would have Dad read the children's books and laugh at his Italian accent: "Jack-a and-a Jill-a run up-a da hill-a, to fetch a pail-a of water." And they're just laughing away at him.

Well, my grandmother Carmela heard about this, and it made her so mad that she ran over to the principal and tore into him: "How dare you make fun of us. We're immigrants. We're new. We're trying to learn the language."

But the principal said to her, "This is America. Learn how to speak English"—just like that.

My grandparents didn't protest. They didn't take it to the superintendent. The principal had a good point, and they knew it.

And you know what? My father was so smart that he became an honor student in school and skipped two grades on his way to graduating from the Newark and Belleville school systems. Dad earned a law degree in 1940, when he was only twenty-four, from the University of Newark Law School (now Rutgers Law School). He became a lawyer known for representing the non-English speaking blue-collar laborers of all ethnicities. That's the Italian way: If you're going to come at us, we're going to come at you ten times harder—and we're always going to come out on top.

But I'm getting ahead of the story. As my dad was about to take his bar exam, the army called him into service for World War II. He finished law school, but the army had other things on their agenda for him. He didn't complain. The army asked him, "What do you do? What kind of job do you have?"

As he had been going through law school, he pumped gas at the station across the street from the house. So he told them he was working at a gas station.

"OK. Good," the army responded. "You're going to put the bombs on the planes because you know about engines."

Wait . . . what?

But that's the way it was.

He was so brilliant. He went on to officer training school and became a second lieutenant. Then they shipped him overseas. They were being careful not to send the boys across the Atlantic and into the German U-boats, so they shipped Pop all the way around the world. He went by way of the West Coast, to Australia, up through Africa, and finally to Taranto, Italy. Before this, he had barely ever been out of New Jersey.

As it turned out, Pop was sent to the Italian provinces of Bari and Foggia. At Bari, he was stationed at what is now called Aviano Air Force Base, which hosts the US Air Force's 31st Fighter Wing. During the war, Pop often drove over to Pratola Serra, and they welcomed him like the hero he was. Aunts, uncles, and cousins lived there—it was a family reunion of sorts. He told me that the Nazis had taken everything from our Piscopo kin: the livestock, the fish, the food. So here you have the Italian descendants—literally, the children of these villages—coming back to the Italian motherland as US soldiers to liberate their families from Mussolini and Hitler.

Eventually, the Army started using Dad's law experience, making him a defense attorney for soldiers charged with minor crimes, like stealing beer. They'd be under a court-martial, but my father got all of them off the charges every time. He got so many guys out of trouble that the army changed course and made him a prosecutor instead.

Dad was gone from home for four and a half years—almost all of it stationed in Italy. I read a letter he wrote his parents at some point during the war, telling them about a request he made:

"I need a break. Some leave time," he told his colonel.

"You want a break?" the colonel replied. "Why don't you tell that to those fellows who just died in the Bataan Death March? A break? I'll give you a break."

Pop wrote, "Needless to say, the colonel got his way. I'm staying here."

Pop's credo—and one that I try to live by—is that he just did what needed to be done. He wasn't looking to be a hero, but he was so good at what he did that the army made a major out of him by the war's end. He never bragged about it. He never complained about it. That generation—God almighty!—they were something else. When I think about all the sacrifices that men and women have made to build this nation and defend her, I can't understand why we now have so many people who just want to throw it all away. Do they even know how good we have it here in America? Do they even know what it took for our ancestors to come to this land and make her so great?

———

The immigrant population in the United States is the foundation of the United States. It's the mosaic, the true fabric of America. But man, oh man, these days, don't ever make fun of anybody's ethnicity. Don't do humor like Don Rickles used to do—holy cannoli, you can't say anything anymore. Frank Sinatra and Dean Martin would go back and forth onstage, calling themselves these racist Italian names—they were Italian, so you dealt with it. But outsiders also felt they could call us Italians all the names they wanted. They could show us in stereotypical portrayals on television—and we had to take that too.

I love my Italian roots. Did I mention that I host the broadcast of the annual Columbus Day Parade in New York City—alongside the talented fellow Italian Maria Bartiromo? And now, every year, we are seeing communities take down statues of Christopher Columbus— one of the most celebrated Italians in world history.

Did you know that one of the largest mass lynchings in America was against eleven Italian Americans in New Orleans in March 1891? In response to the murder of the police commissioner, a mob raided the jail and went after Sicilians who had been rounded up. They strung them up on lampposts. *The New York Times* published a fake news story about the lynchings with a front-page headline that approved of it: "Chief Hennessy Avenged: Eleven of His Italian Assassins Lynched by a Mob" and "An Uprising of Indignant Citizens in New Orleans—The Prison Doors Forced and the Italian Murderers Shot Down."[4] In 2019, the mayor of New Orleans apologized for the injustice—almost 130 years after the fact.[5]

Recently, I had the chance to talk to a woman from Jamaica who works hard to help senior adults in their homes. She has gotten her green card and is working through the process of becoming a citizen. It costs her a lot of time and resources, but she wants to do it. She wants to become a citizen of the United States. I told her about how the Italians throughout the first half of the twentieth century were in the same position—working hard to become part of this great nation.

Many of my parents' generation of Italians were the entertainers for America: Dean Martin (birth name Dino Paul Crocetti), Frank Sinatra, Bobby Darin (birth name Walden Robert Cassotto), Julius La Rosa—we owned it. We were the immigrants who came to America with songs in our hearts, a good set of pipes, and last names ending with vowels. The culture said, "Oh, look at those Italians. Look at them sing. If they're not gangsters, they're singing." That was the idea. The best singers were all Italian. And the best comedians were Jewish. That's what they said—literally. In 1978, *TIME* magazine claimed that 80 percent of professional comedians in America were Jewish.[6]

My grandparents lived in the Italian neighborhood that inter-sected with the Jewish neighborhood. In my career, I guess I've always been at that intersection too—straddling the line between comedy and music. I consider myself a blue-collar entertainer, a working stiff who loves this country and its people.

My father and uncle—gifted as they were with amazing minds—worked hard to get educated. My pop became a lawyer. My Uncle Ben was a chemical engineer, working with Enrico Fermi to develop the nuclear program for this country. They were proud to be American. They didn't land on the shores and start in with "I hate America" or "Let's change this country." Change it into what? Change it into the place you just fled from? No, the Piscopos *kept* their heritage *and also* became proud Americans.

There you have it. Even though almost all of my grandparents' generation was born in Italy, by the time I showed up in 1951, it was all about Newark, New Jersey, baby.

God bless America.

2

JERSEY BOY

Before she married, my mom worked as a bookkeeper for her brothers who had an electronics manufacturing business. During the war, they made radios and other electronic devices that they would load onto the train right there outside of Newark and ship to the government.

When Pop came back home from the war, he met my mother and fell in love. They married in 1946 and moved just a few blocks away from his parents in Belleville, a suburb of Newark. For about $8,000 they bought 10 Copper Place, a tiny house of 1,100 square feet built in 1947—a true GI Bill house.

If you've seen *Jersey Boys*, then you've seen Belleville. Copper Place sat just across Branch Brook Park from the public housing that Franki Valli grew up in during the 1940s and lived in until 1964—two years after "Sherry" became a #1 Billboard hit. In fact, actor Joe Pesci graduated from Belleville High School. As a teenager, Pesci introduced Valli and Tommy DeVito to Bob Gaudio, the singer and songwriter who helped transform them into The Four Seasons. Anyhow, that's where my folks lived when I came into the world on June 17, 1951, at Passaic General Hospital.

In 1953, when I was two years old, my parents moved us a few miles north of Belleville to Bloomfield, another suburb of Newark. We lived right on the cusp of Brookdale Park for about ten years, and living there impacted my childhood in the best way possible.

I had an idyllic childhood. Even today, whenever I drive through Bloomfield and Belleville, I call my mother just to thank her for allowing us such a great childhood. We had a park, playgrounds, piano lessons, baseball fields, schools we walked to, and safety—it was Norman Rockwell. You just feel grateful for what you were given.

Steve Martin wrote about his icy and tense relationship with his father: "I have heard it said that a complicated childhood can lead to a life in the arts. I tell you this story of my father and me to let you know I am qualified to be a comedian."[7] In his memoirs, fellow New Jersey boy Bruce Springsteen also wrote of home-life angst. But my childhood and relationship with my parents cannot be described in those terms. My life as a Jersey boy had a *Leave It to Beaver* dynamic— though mine was filled with lots of pasta, loud aunts and uncles, and going to Mass.

I've got a sister and a brother. My sister, Carol, is eighteen months older than I am, and my brother, Richie, is eighteen months younger. I was the middle child who got the blame for everything. My father would be driving us around in his Oldsmobile. I'd be in the middle of the backseat, with my sister on my right and Richie directly behind Dad. So, if we were goofing around, my Pop—he could be quick—would just turn backward and smack me so fast. And it wasn't even my fault! I was an angel, you see. I'd think (but not say), *It wasn't me, Pop*—but boom!—that was it. And you kept your mouth shut. Nothing like, "Oh, Dad, it was Richie." None of that. It was *respect your father*. And a smack was the consequence for being a wise guy.

Don't get me wrong—my parents were good to us. Incredible parents who loved us and provided for us. I remember having a little bike that was OK, but I got my heart set on having a Schwinn. Not just a beautiful Schwinn bike but the kind with hand brakes on each side of the handlebars. I didn't want the foot brakes anymore because as you got older, it was cooler to have the hand brakes. As you coasted down the hill, you could kind of back-pedal, and that click-click-click-click-click-click sound was cool. And then you could slow yourself down with the hand brakes—so sophisticated, right? So, one Christmas, my parents got me a great Schwinn bike, but it had only one hand brake and still had foot brakes. I didn't want to be a brat and show on my face what I was thinking in my mind. I probably did, though—and here it is, some sixty years later, and I can still remember that moment.

I attended Brookdale Elementary School in Bloomfield, which you could walk to in ten minutes from our house. And as you did, you'd pass by Holsten's Ice Cream shop—the actual diner where they filmed the final scene of *The Sopranos*.

Judge Andrew Napolitano went there, too, though he's one year older than I am. I remember us walking around the playground—Johnny Vargo, me, Kenny Russo, and Napolitano. Nap, as we called him, would always be walking with his hands behind his back. He was always studying—very academic. So it was no surprise when he became the youngest judge on the Superior Court in New Jersey.

Brookdale Park was an oasis for me as a kid. I have the fondest memories of playing there all the time with my friends and my cousin Paulie. We would play baseball. We would climb trees. We would go down Snake Hill on bikes in the summer and sleds in the winter. Another hill was called Suicide Hill. I remember my brother crashing once and ripping his lip open. Great memories. All day long, we would play there. It was safe. Your parents didn't have to worry about anything back then—and we kids certainly didn't worry.

Don't tell me about privilege. How dare you say that! For Mom and Pop, it was just hard work that got them there. Hard work.

Mom is the one who enlightened me in faith and religion. She's a stellar human, leading me and those she came in contact with toward the path to Jesus. I'm biased because she's my mom, but I just don't know that people are like her anymore. The way she would get up real early, get us out to school, take care of my pop, and then entertain on the weekends. Amazing stamina. And always putting forth the most effort and energy and thoughtfulness for her family.

My mother would make a sit-down dinner every Sunday afternoon. When we got out of bed on Sundays, she would say, "You can't eat," because we had to go to church, and you couldn't eat before communion back then. So we would go to church and take communion. Then my mother would come home and make pancakes. To this day, you can smell Ma and Grandma's pancakes. My mom—I loved her. And then we would all play baseball outside, dressed up and all, and then she'd call us inside for lunch. If it was 2:00 p.m. on Sunday, then you can bet there would be an entire pot roast ready to be eaten, with pasta on the side. The dining room table would be covered with a stark white tablecloth. And after we ate all this good food, there would be a nap—at least among the adults.

————

On Christmas Eve we ate fish. It's a tradition called the Feast of Seven Fishes. It's more religious than superstition, but it's bad luck if you don't have fish on Christmas Eve. It's sacrilegious even. My mother would make seared scallops—perfectly seared scallops—and then she would always make flounder. Then you would have shrimp, you would have mussels, you had clams, and you'd maybe have a seafood salad, as it were, with some scungilli. I remember as a child going into my grandmother's kitchen on Christmas Eve, seeing there were octopus tentacles hanging out of the boiling pot, and thinking, *Oh my gosh! Who are these people? How barbaric is this? You're boiling an octopus!* But yeah, you'd eat it and all the other dishes of seven fishes. That was the Italian way.

Of course, I had friends who were Jewish and other ethnicities, and it seemed like we all had our traditions that centered on family and food. I believe you should take pride in what your ethnicity is because ethnicity is the foundation of America. We should remember the legacy of our foremothers and forefathers because that's what makes the country stronger.

Father Knows Best

My father was the most intelligent man I've ever met. Smart. When I would do homework in high school, I didn't have to go to the Encyclopedia Britannica. I would ask Dad. He knew every answer to every question of any category on planet Earth. Everything! I've never seen such knowledge with anyone else, and he never even knew it—never knew how smart he was. He just did it.

Dad compartmentalized his feelings like so many of his generation. Those fathers loved us, but they'd never tell you they loved you when you were a kid. And Pop was very strict. Like I said, if I did something bad, he would just smack me. That was his generation.

My father worked in Passaic as a compensation attorney. He went out independently in 1957 and started a small operation. It wasn't a big law firm. He was a single lawyer representing a lot of work-related injuries. Historically, the textile factories in Passaic employed endless streams of immigrants from dozens of nations. The working conditions and low pay led to strikes and labor strife in the early part of the century. These events tied into my father's law career because he became a pioneer in fighting for workers' rights, using his God-given smarts for the betterment of blue-collar workers from every ethnic background. My father represented many Polish Americans who had just come to the US and couldn't speak the language yet. They'd get hurt on the job, and the insurance companies wouldn't give them justice until my pop stood up and fought for them.

I remember once he defended this guy who got his thumb sliced off while working at the Empire State Building. Missing a thumb handicaps anyone, especially a blue-collar worker who uses his hands all day to get the job done. But Pop had to fight to get this man good compensation. He took me to court with him that day—I must have been about ten years old. The lawyers from the other side had the man hold up his noninjured hand as they made their case for a lesser amount of money: "He's got another thumb, your Honor. Here's a perfectly good thumb."

My father was like, "Are you kidding me? That's not an argument." Pop fought hard and won the injured man some justice. When you faced my dad in court, you could expect he'd put the thumbs on you.

———

People ask me if I came from a family with humor. Yes, definitely. My father was very funny. Always. He was hysterical. He knew more jokes and could tell them with perfect delivery—*bada bing, bada boom*—better than anyone I've ever heard professionally. No matter how tough the situation, my dad would laugh about it. He would always take a lighthearted approach. It's a great survival skill, and I think I definitely picked it up from him. Everything was funny to Dad, no matter what.

It got so that when Pop went into court and would be in the holding place for the attorneys, standing there with all the other lawyers, waiting for their case to be called, the bailiff would come over and say quietly, "Mr. Piscopo, the judge wants to see you in his chambers." The judge would call Pop back there just to hear the latest jokes. Of course, the material was all politically incorrect—clean-cut entertainment.

Besides the punch-line jokes, Dad's career provided real-life humorous fodder. Not that I directly used these experiences in sketches, but they gave me the ability to see humor in everyday life, even in violent or morbid happenings. And at least once, the violence was aimed at Dad himself.

My father had a client who had gotten hurt on the job as a grave digger. My father took the case when no one else would. So, one night at home, the week before Christmas in 1962, Pop was late, and we couldn't figure out where he could be. Why wasn't he home? Turns out this former client went delusional, thinking my dad had not gotten him a good enough settlement. Pop was walking across the street close to his office in Passaic. He had just come out of his offices, located in the tallest building in Passaic (then called the County Bank Building), and was on his way to his car.[8] He turned sideways a bit as he reached into his pocket because it suddenly occurred to him that he needed to buy some cigarettes on the way home. Thinking about his smokes probably saved his life because right as he turned around, this client of his was in the process of shooting at Pop from a moving car. He hit Dad three times—in the arm, the leg, and the stomach—with a .25-caliber French gun he had bought a month earlier.

I was ten years old at the time, and I remember the police standing at the door of our house. I was behind my mother's apron strings, literally, and I could see the officer's revolver—probably a .38-caliber—and all those bullets on his belt.

The officer said something comforting: "Mrs. Piscopo, your husband is doing OK. He got shot, and we're here to take you to the hospital."

Within minutes, my Aunt Louise came over. We were all so close in every sense of the word. I remember my mother going out the door. I was down on my knees, praying to God, "Please don't take my father."

Everyone was running around, the kids excited because of all the publicity of it. And Pop pulled through. The bullet was lodged in his stomach, but he was a warrior.

My cousin Pat came in and said, "Hey, your dad is on the radio. He's on the radio, Joe."

I said, "Yeah, well, you go ahead and listen. I've got some things to settle here." I had been praying for my dad to survive. Now, I prayed a word of thanks to God.

It's amazing how differently my entire life would have been had the guy actually killed Pop. I mean, I was just ten. That would have changed everything. But God kept him alive that day and for forty more years. To the day that he died, a piece of shrapnel remained lodged in his left leg. That he survived gives me great humility to God and gratitude for all those who have lost their lives serving and protecting me—all of us—in the line of duty and in defense of our country. I keep my faith in God because of it. And my respect for law enforcement too.

The story ran in the local papers off and on for years, as the crazy man went to trial and then was committed to a mental institution. And then, years later, the story of the shooting reemerged as the man came up for release. Every time he was in the news, the story of Dad getting shot came back into print. I suppose it was good for his business, though. I can hear people thinking, *That Piscopo must be a tough you know what. His own client shot him three times, and he was out of the hospital in a week.*

Seriously, though, this one event made my father famous, but it also made people think that my dad had pissed off the wrong people: "Someone tried to whack that Italian lawyer Piscopo." That's the first time I heard about all that stuff, the idea that we were all connected to gangsters and the stuff you'd see later in all the movies. The truth is 99.9 percent of Italian Americans have never even met a gangster. Still, when your dad gets shot in the streets, it gets people talking and saying things that have no bearing on reality.

There's a postscript to this story that shows my dad's sense of humor. In 1970, Dad was interviewed by a newspaper:

> Joseph Piscopo of Passaic says the funniest thing that ever happened to him was when he got shot on the street by one of his clients. He had gotten some workmen's compensation for this client, but the man didn't think it was enough, so he shot his lawyer. A lot of people have thought of doing this, but few actually do it.
>
> "This really slayed me," says Joe.
>
> Incidentally, the man was an unemployed gravedigger. [8]

That's my Pop. In my mind, I can still see the bullet that they pulled out of him, and it's all a traumatic memory. But Dad? He always had a keen sense of humor about stuff like this. It was just his way of dealing with life.

———

I found another newspaper clipping, this one from the October 26, 1960, edition of Passaic's *Herald-News,* telling how my dad represented a newlywed couple who was suing the owner of the Peter Pan Motel.

> The complaint, drawn by Joseph P. Piscopo, Passaic attorney, charges the motel management with negligence in permitting private detectives to raid the place.
>
> La Corte [the groom] also said that in trying to prevent private detectives from entering the cabin, he was physically assaulted. . . .
>
> Their attorney says in the papers that the 3 a.m. raid occurred on the couple's first day of their honeymoon. La Corte had been home on leave from the army.
>
> Piscopo said the raiders had been following a philandering husband and had picked the La Corte cabin by mistake. [9]

Did you catch all that? First night of the marriage. While on leave from the army. At 3 a.m., some private detectives looking for a "philandering husband" got their wires crossed about either the groom or the room. They busted in the door and busted up the young couple's first night together. As the title of the Dean Martin and Sammy Cahn song from that year said, "Ain't That a Kick in the Head." And there was my pop, representing the honeymooners in court to get them some justice for the awful interruption.

Here's another gem of a case my dad took on. The *Herald-News*, dated April 22, 1961, published this headline: "Blistered Shoe Buyer Sues the Shoe Store." The plaintiff said he bought a pair of shoes at Prozy's on May 1, 1959. They didn't fit. He returned them and got another pair, and that pair gave him a blister, requiring medical attention. So he had my dad file a lawsuit against the shoe store—two years later!

Can you even imagine how little the payout must have been for my dad for this kind of work? What would he earn? A pair of wingtips? A case of shoe polish? Pop always said he would nickel and dime his way to fees as a lawyer because he never charged a lot of money. That's why I use that term now in what I do as an entertainer. I nickel and dime my way through the year—always working. Never stopping. Sweating to entertain ordinary, everyday people.

There were dozens of his cases that made it into the local paper— out of hundreds and hundreds of clients he served during his career. I mention these because they're funny. But the vast majority of his clients were involved in tragic accidents at work or negligent behavior that injured people. You can't make up stuff like this—real-life pains and sorrows—and my pop was right there in the mix of it all, coming to the aid of everyday people needing legal help.

When my dad died in 2002, so many people came to see him at his wake—lots of people I had never met. I looked up and saw this guy come in the door, an ethnic minority with dirt on his fingers and on his jeans. It was obvious that he had just gotten off work.

"Can I help you?" I asked.

"I just wanted to pay respect to your dad," he replied. "I'm a trucker. A few years ago, my back got hurt bad while on the job. I wasn't able to work for a while, and I couldn't get a dime. But your father got me the money I deserved, and it got me back on my feet. It's how I survived."

That was my dad—God rest his soul.

A Star Is Born

When I was in third and fourth grades, all I wanted to do was play baseball in Bloomfield Park with Johnny Vargo and the guys. But my mother insisted I take piano lessons from Mrs. Gimble up in Glen Ridge.

"You have to take piano because you have a knack for music, Joe," she said.

So my parents bought a piano, and Mrs. Gimble started her work turning me into Beethoven. Pretty soon, it was time for a recital, so Mrs. Gimble had us all playing pieces with Mexican themes. And for some scenery, she placed a wooden burro onstage. Because, you know, to a bunch of New Jersey Italians in 1960, one look at a wooden donkey let everyone know they'd be hearing some mighty fine Spanish music before the day ended.

Each of us did our number and then walked backstage. The next group was ready to go out, but Mrs. Gimble said, "Oh no! I left the donkey on the stage."

Without missing a beat, I said, "I'll go get it. Not a problem."

I turned and walked back out onstage in front of all the parents. With all eyes watching me, I sauntered over to the prop, held my hands up with my fingers together in the Italian manner (Google

"Italian hand emoji"), and said to the donkey, "Ey, wadda ya doin'? What's the matter with you?"

The place exploded with laughter. Screams. Brought the house down. When you're in third grade and do this kind of thing and get big laughs, I really dug it. I've never forgotten that moment or the feeling I got. The memory is indelible, imprinted on my brain forever. That moment onstage with Mrs. Gimble must have been my first foray into the feeling that comes with approval from an audience. And I was hooked.

It's been sixty years since I took those lessons and sixty years of performing music live and making people laugh, so I really should pause here and just say, "Mom, you were right. Thanks!"

I remember watching Guy Marks (if you don't know him, you'll want to Google him—trust me) on *The Ed Sullivan Show* and thinking that I wanted to be just like him. That's like a young baseball player saying he wants to be the next Bob Uecker. I never wanted to be a star. I never thought about it that way. I just wanted to work. Marks would do characters and trick songs—bits and voices. Guys like that could hold my attention for a while. I enjoyed the actual comedians—the Allen Kings and Jackie Masons—but I didn't want to be a comic. I wanted to be a character—an entertainer who did pieces. I was just so enthralled with that.

———

It was the 1950s, and America owned it. It was great. We were powerful. Eisenhower was the president. And all I remember was how great America was. That's certainly what my father told me—how great America was and how great the United States Army was. He would teach me all the military drills, complete with a toy bolt-action rifle. Pop was just so in love with this country, and that's where I am today. He's been gone for over twenty years, but I still share that belief with Pop.

People misunderstand me when I say that because they think it means I was indoctrinated. It's not that at all. Pop just showed me the beauty of this land and our nation's history and government and freedoms. My mother enlightened me to the beauty of the Lord, and her faith is unwavering—as mine is. That is my mom. And my love of the country comes from my father. That's not indoctrination; it's passing along a love.

Therein lies my impetus for living like I am now—trying to help people and causes that can impact lives one at a time. My pop's commitments as a lawyer. My mother's commitment to God, the church, and Christ. Everything I say about my parents, I appreciated it but never lived it out back then. I guess that's what youth is all about, but ouch!—what missed opportunities. Anyhow, now I can live it out in my work and life.

Yes, I went wayward as a teenager and was so stupid in high school. What was I thinking? But that's the story of the next chapter.

3

AMERICAN PASTORAL

As beautiful as Bloomfield was, my parents continued to have the thought that immigrants have: *What could we do to better ourselves?* My parents announced to us, "We're going to go up Bloomfield Avenue." Apparently, drugs started coming out into the culture, and there were some incidents in Bloomfield Park.

So we moved up the road to North Caldwell sometime in 1963. I know this because I have a memory of my mom picking me up from my new school on the day when President Kennedy was shot in November 1963. People say that his murder marked a turning point, a disillusionment, for older Baby Boomers, those born right after the war who were young adults at the time of the assassination. But I was only twelve, and sorrowful as I was, the event did not crack apart the rosy view of the world that I had at the time. I was focused on fitting in and getting along at the new school.

I was very upset about leaving Bloomfield because all my friends were there. Who wants to go to a new place? I was all set to go to a school in Bloomfield (which isn't there now) called North Junior High

School. And then I would have gone to Bloomfield High School. I knew exactly what my life was going to look like for the next six years and was all excited about that.

But to show you how great my dad was—as we were in the process of moving, for the first six weeks of school, Pop took us back and forth. They didn't want us to start at one school and then switch right in the middle of the first quarter. Father knows best, right? It was at least a twenty-five-minute drive, and then Pop had to go from there to Passaic to his office or court. I remember it like it was yesterday too. He would get in his car. He'd have his Parliament cigarette in the ashtray. We had the radio set to WNEW, listening to music all the way. I loved radio and still do—and some of that love goes back to riding in the car with Pop. That's how I learned to be a dad, because he was a great one. When he got upset, he got upset. I mean, he didn't want any messing around. But the commitment he had to us was just incredible. Driving us, that was a lot to do—and he did it. Didn't even think about doing anything else. Pop went to that length to do that for us.

———

If you Google "North Caldwell," you'll first discover that the fictional Tony Soprano's real-life house is in this township. But when we moved to North Caldwell, it wasn't like that yet. It wasn't full of those big Tony Soprano houses—all that unfolded after I left.

Now, don't get me wrong. This entire area was beautiful and suburban. But we weren't wealthy like the people in the next township over, Essex Fells. That was where the real elites lived. I would date the really rich, suburban, elite girls from Essex Fells. They all had one thing none of us North Caldwell folks had: color television. I remember being so amazed at that. I'd be at these friends' houses watching their color TV, and they'd be ready to go, but I'd say, "Yeah, sure. I'll be with you in a minute guys. This is so cool."

So Pop bought the place in 1963, a brand new home with 1,600 square feet and a third of an acre. My father would always tell me that measurement—a third of an acre—because that was a lot of land for a guy who came from Newark. He was proud of it.

When my grandfather would come out to the place, he would look around the yard and start pointing. With his heavy Italian accent, he would say to my dad, "You should put-a another house-a there," or "You're not growing olives? You should be growing olives or oranges—or something."

They were farmers in the old world. That's what my people were. Or, in town, they were blacksmiths. It's a beautiful town with delightful people and gorgeous fields all around.

Wealth and affluence. It's all so relative, you know.

Anyhow, six decades later, my mom still lived in the same house until she passed away in December 2023. How's that for stability, clean living, and strong genes?

West Essex High School

I went to West Essex High School from seventh grade through high school graduation. It was awful—at least at first. I mean, it was a great school for some, but not for me because it was seven through twelve, all those grades thrown together. And I was a new kid in the area. Now I'm in a new school—new to me and relatively new itself. I was so insecure. I was going through puberty. My elementary school friends were all back in Bloomfield. Who were all these new people? This just seemed like a bad idea.

With all the Baby Boomer generation needing classroom space, the powers that be opened this "regional" school in 1960, consisting of kids from four townships: Essex Fells, Roseland, Fairfield, and North Caldwell. Let's just say that we came from different socioeconomic backgrounds, so when I showed up in 1963 as a seventh grader, it was culture shock compared to the comfortable environs of Bloomfield. David Chase, the creator of *The Sopranos*, graduated from West Essex a few years before me, and he used familiar surroundings for his material. So this is the same high school that Tony Soprano fictionally attended, where he played football and baseball and met his future bride, Carmela.

During my second week at West Essex, I'm in the hallway, which is jammed and crowded with flocks of pimple-faced, adolescent Baby Boomers. One guy, an eighth grader, is pushing through the mass of adolescents and shouting, "Seventh graders! Out of the way."

So what do I do? Do I get out of the way? No. I say, "Hey, let's get him, guys." I just say those words before I can think to do otherwise.

He turns. Big kid. Huge kid. He says, "Yeah?" and comes after me. "Want to do something about it?"

Now, there's a circle of kids. Spectators. Everyone wants to see the bloodbath dished out on this new kid.

Well, I just did what my father told me to do in such a situation: Go into a boxing stance. Pop always taught Richie and me how to box. How to stay put, to lessen your target. Kind of like the martial arts I would learn later in prep for fighting Chuck Norris onscreen (more on that later). That's what I did with this big bully. He kept trying to hit me with haymakers. I'd duck and then—pop!—I'd get in a punch while he was swinging through and missing me. I made him bleed. I totally got the best of him.

Of course, now I was known. So much for keeping my head low in the new school.

The adults broke up the fight and took us into the boys' room to clean up this kid and his bloody face.

"What's your name?" I asked.

"Claude Stiletto," he blubbered.

Seriously. The guy's last name was Stiletto.

"Where you from?" I asked.

"Bloomfield."

"You're from Bloomfield?" I said. "You're Italian?"

"Yeah, of course, I'm Italian," he said. And with that, I'd made a new friend. We're Italian. So we were friends now, and it was OK. We settled it.

Next thing you know, it's lunch. Claude Stiletto comes over to the table where I'm sitting with my new classmates. Stiletto says loudly, where everyone can hear, "Hey, Piscopo can handle himself. Look at this kid. He's alright."

But later that day, Stiletto reversed course and decided I needed a pummeling after all. "You and me. Outside the gym. After school."

I'm not a tough guy, you know, but I'm the new kid, and I can't back down. So after-school plans are set for Round 2.

By the end of the day, the whole school knows about it. We're out there. I'm saying, "Look, I don't want to fight. I don't want to fight."

"Oh, you're chicken?"

"No, I just don't want to fight."

"Take your rings off," he says, ignoring my pacifism. That was the rule—no rings. Off came my confirmation ring.

Stiletto comes at me and my father's coaching had prepared me well. I'm throwing jabs, one after another. I hit him smack dab in the kisser. The poor kid is bleeding all over. Then, I circle around, grab him from behind, and just start slamming him against the door to the gym. One of the football players comes out, and every time I slam Stiletto, the football player pushes him back toward me. The original Italian Stallion, that's me.

Well, that turned into my first suspension. Boom. Second week of school.

––––––––––

The problem was I couldn't stand being in a classroom. Nowadays, they would say, "Oh, he's got ADHD"—and I believe it. My friends say I've got it even now. My poor mother, God bless her, would get all those phone calls from the school office: "Your son was fighting again."

I was always doing dumb stuff in school to get a laugh. One day in biology class, we dissected a frog. I had my turn making cuts and looking at guts, and I knew we were about to go back to our seats, so I crawled into one of the cabinets. I just snuck in, hid, and waited. The teacher called the class to order and started up his lecture about the amazing leg muscles of these amphibians and how far they could jump. I took that as my cue and jumped out of the cabinet: Joe Piscopo, at your service for a laugh. Boom—Piscopo, report to the office. Boom—Piscopo, you're suspended . . . again. Anything for a laugh.

Life Saver

It was in high school where I really fell in love with performing. That's when I knew where my heart was taking me. As I began to get into trouble in seventh and eighth grades, I started playing in the band and started playing rock and roll. Then my sister said, "You know, there's a drama department here. You may like being onstage." My first thought was that there was no way I would do that. But thank God for sisters. Truly, what a good piece of advice that turned out to be.

I met the school's drama and debate coach, Mr. Gauntt. I say this with the greatest of love, and I miss him every day, but he was the most flaming and flamboyant guy—and this is in the mid-1960s! But he was so grand in all that he did. We all thought, *Who is this guy?* You know, because we all considered ourselves tough kids and jocks. But Mr. Gauntt was such a great mentor to all of us. He told us to straighten up. He challenged our self-perception as tough guys by telling us to learn our lines and recite them onstage in front of several hundred people. If we could do *that*, then we could call ourselves tough.

Chuck was a take-no-prisoners, tough-as-nails director and producer of the shows. And he was a great actor in his own right, starring in community plays. He became our mentor and boss.

Years later, I created a character, Charles E. Blunt, for an *SNL* sketch, based on my memory of Charles E. Gauntt. The character was a drama coach, and the sketch worked well, but it may have been ahead of its time.

To all of us who were hopelessly hetero and somewhat jocks, Chuck came from another lifestyle—another world altogether. He absolutely loved and emulated the flamboyant English playwright and actor Noel Coward (you'll want to YouTube "Noel Coward" to see what I'm saying). He wore ascots and vests and always spoke dramatically with a big, booming voice. I think we all loved him because he was so against authority. Given how conservative things still were in the mid-1960s, he said some of the wildest things, like: "Oh, I think I'll just go home on the back porch and sip a gin and tonic stark naked." That kind of stuff would get you arrested nowadays, but we just thought it was incredibly fun back then.

He was so different from us, but he had our immense respect because he was so talented and cared about us. He understood the problem teen that I had become. I remember screwing around one day. I had decided to cut a class by going up to this place backstage where all the lights were run. Unbeknownst to me, Chuck saw me sneaking in. I can still hear his baritone voice belting out theatrically, "Joey, what the *hell* do you think you are doing?"

"Ah, Chuck, I need a break," I shouted back. "I'm just going to hang out for a while."

He goes, "Oh hell. Well, I didn't see you." And he spoke the words like they were the last lines of a Shakespearean tragedy.

———

I'm not being dramatic when I say this, but I believe drama saved my life. It gave me a focus beyond just goofing off. Through the performing arts in high school, I found myself. I lived for it. I couldn't do school well, but drama straightened me out. You learned your words and executed them onstage properly. By the grace of God only, you could command the crowd's attention. You could control it. I was so insecure. Personally, I think every performer is insecure; they go out there for approval. That's my armchair-psychologist take on it. You're asking the crowd, "You like me, right?" Every single show is just that—you're seeking approval. On the other hand, your ego is such that you are sure of yourself, and you find your comfort zone onstage. That's where I found mine. To this day, I'm most comfortable onstage in front of a vast audience. Isn't that weird?

And it's also where I learned that I have an insatiable curiosity for the everyman—and that has impacted me greatly in my life and career. When I meet people, I think, *I want to hear your story. Tell me your story.* That curiosity has to be an instinct.

———

I acted in my first play as a sophomore, a one-act called *The Jury*, where I played the judge. Sophomores were expected to do the one-acts and other light work. And if you were any good, then you would hope to be in the big productions as a junior or senior.

The first play I did on the big stage was called *Gramercy Ghost*, where I played the ghost—halo, sheet, and all. It was as embarrassing as it sounds, but I told myself I was paying my dues. You fall in love with acting and being onstage. But you have to go through the minor leagues first. You had to be part of a drama group, and then as you got older, you'd audition for the major productions.

I played the role of Chick Clark in *My Sister Eileen*, and after that, Chuck told me I'd be playing the lead role—Joe Hardy—in the next semester's big production of *Damn Yankees*. What a thrill it was to have found something I was good at and enjoyed. It seemed like I had turned around my high school career after all.

After all that acting, I was fortunate to receive the Lincoln Center Student Arts Award. They picked three students from our school and other schools in the tri-state areas of New York, New Jersey, and Connecticut and sent us to the Lincoln Center to see Shakespeare's *King Lear*. There, on the stage of the beautiful Vivian Beaumont Theater, the legendary actor Lee J. Cobb mesmerized me with his performance in the lead role. I was just blown away. I walked out that night just thinking differently about what I would or could do in life.

Driving & Down the Shore

Like most Baby Boomer teens, I loved cars, and I loved the beach.

I got my driver's permit at sixteen and my license at seventeen. We drove my parents' cars, which at first was an Oldsmobile 98. My father got a beautiful Chrysler 300, but then, in 1964, he got a Cadillac. I remember thinking, *Wow, Dad's got a Caddy*.

Uncle Ben gave me a 1963 Imperial, a truly classic car. I kick myself every day because I should have held on to that beauty. Black paint and red interior, with turnout seats and a push-button transmission— what a car! I'd also take my mom's Oldsmobile 98 when I had a date. I'd roll into neighboring Essex Fells to see some wealthy friends. Their families drove foreign cars, and I never understood why. "My dad just paid twenty grand for that Mercedes," they would tell me, but I would just scratch my head. The fancy American cars we bought only cost three to five grand.

Later, my Father set me up with Mom's 1972 Olds Cutlass. I don't even think I paid him for it—God bless him. That was my first car of my own. A few years later, I bought myself a Ford Fairmont and was proud of that set of wheels until the day I pulled up to the curb to pick up some of the guys.

Jerry Seinfeld looked at my Fairmont and laughed. "Joe, that looks like a United States government vehicle." I don't know what he was driving back then when he hadn't yet broke, but he went on to own fifty Porsches.

Still, that Fairmont was a gem, baby.

———————

Every summer, my family would go "down the shore," that is, the Jersey Shore. Our family would rent a house in Lavallette, New Jersey, part of the coastline that's just north of Seaside Heights, where MTV filmed the *Jersey Shore* reality TV show (with a bunch of actors from New York). We would go to all the places Pop had visited as a kid. We never wanted to leave.

One year, we rented a place further south on Long Beach Island. Just two hours south of North Caldwell, right down the Garden State Parkway along the coast. We loved it so much, and at the end of our stay, Pop said we could stay longer, but we had to move to a different house because the one we were in was already rented out.

Then I remember him being at the top of the beach one day, talking with a friend of his and pointing: "That house right there. Yeah, I think I'm going to get that house." And he did! With $100 down, literally. It was an $11,000 house—this was in the late 1950s. A little post–World War II cottage in Beach Haven. Exactly what it still is to this day. Our family still owns it. I've been going down there for most of my life now. Same house!

As you can imagine, the whole area kept getting developed, but our block on 12th Street is pretty much the same. The nouveau riche come down, and they build the big new things.

I would fly into Atlantic City for a show, and afterward, I would be driven down to our place. The limo service would pull up to Long Beach Island, and as you go over the causeway onto the island, you had to turn to the left or to the right. The really rich were north—to the left—big mansions and all.

The driver would say, "To the left, Mr. Piscopo?"

I would laugh. "No, pal, to the right. You see that Ferris wheel by the amusement park? That's where we are. Down that way, man."

It was really blue-collar. The houses were so close together. They're still like that. I always identify with that. That's the heart of my parents. And I'm still best friends with all my buddies from that area.

Once Pop bought the house in Beach Haven, we didn't just vacation there for a week or two. We lived there the entire summer. The day school ended, we packed up and left for Beach Haven. I remember one year we got up at five in the morning and left our summer beach home on the first day of school. We just drove on in and started school on the same day, having sucked every last minute out of our summer fun at the beach.

Of course, Pop didn't stay at Beach Haven all week. He would stay back and work, then drive down on the weekends. The courts closed in August, so he could get out of the office on Wednesday or Thursday and enjoy a long weekend.

I'm not going to use the word *privileged* to describe my parents, because they both worked real hard to get what they were able to give us. They were good, God-fearing, America-loving citizens who wanted to provide us with a good life. And they did. Their hard work allowed us, their children, to be privileged.

When you spend entire summers in one place, it becomes a second home to you, and the people you get to know become friends for life. All the locals were our friends. When I broke out on *Saturday Night Live*, people would come around our house. It was no secret that the Piscopos had this little house in Beach Haven. I still keep up with those guys.

The late Bob Dole used to talk about how when he would go back to Kansas and enter the old house where he was born and raised, he would gain strength there. I know exactly what he meant. That's what happens still when I go to our house in Beach Haven. I sit there where

I once sat with my father, talking and knowing him. I have a picture of my father walking around that house—the knotty pine on the walls. It was another part of what I knew as home.

Nowadays, everybody has got brand new McMansions everywhere on the island. They've built up the whole place, and everything is beautiful and modern. But my mother kept our place just the way it was. It's funny because the land was still open when we first came and we could have spread out a bit more. But we didn't. We just crammed in down there and still do. It's a Jersey thing, man—something that only Jersey folks would understand.

I can't tell you how much I love the ocean there, the water, the beauty, the family. We've been there when it was beautiful and clean. I have happy memories from when dolphins swam along the coastline to sad memories when there were hypodermic needles washing up on the beach in the 1980s. I made a lot of jokes about it back then, but thank God they've cleaned it all up again. Jersey Shore is a beautiful place.

Hey Gyp and James Brown

I had a rock and roll band, mostly in the tenth and eleventh grades. I know that "he who humbles himself is exalted," but I have to say—we were pretty darn good.

It was after the Beatles broke. Beatlemania was running hot, and when they'd be on TV, you always see them with a Vox guitar. I knew where I could get a VOX guitar like that from Caldwell Music Shop. I wanted that guitar so bad, to learn to play rock and roll. On Christmas Day in 1965, Mom made it happen. And the following year, she got me a Fender Vibrolux amp to go along with it.

None of that came cheap even in those days, but Mom knew I was serious about it. And to this day, I have the same Vox guitar and will rehearse with it. I sat with my mom shortly before she died and had the guitar with me. I started playing it and singing songs I had written.

My mother turned to me and said, "You know, you're very good at the guitar. You're very good."

I said, "Ma, you got me the guitar."

That was a special moment. That toy, that guitar, was really *the* Christmas gift for me. I cherish it to this day.

I was the lead singer in the band. John Welshons, one of my best friends, became my bass player. And my drummer was Johnny Vargo, the leader of the pack I was in back at Brookdale Elementary School. Ron Pitts was on guitar. And my friend Richie Mears had a P3 Hammond organ that he could rock.

We called ourselves "Hey Gyp," named after the song made famous by my favorite group, Eric Burdon and the Animals. We played James Brown and the Dave Clark Five.

We practiced all the time, and then we went around playing gigs. We got hired to do dances where we played the Rolling Stones, the Animals, the Beatles—all the standards. We mixed in Dave Clark Five songs with covers of James Brown. We were good, and we had so much fun. I loved performing onstage, singing, and helping people have a good time. And fifty years later, I still love doing live performances.

———

Speaking of James Brown, I saw so many amazing musical artists in the four years I was on *SNL*. So naturally, I've been asked many times, "Who was it that just blew your mind?" The answer: James Brown—and here's why.

In July 1967, as a sophomore in high school, I went to the riots in my parents' hometown in Newark, New Jersey. We saw the city burn down. Afterward, all the politicians came out in force—the social justice warriors of the day. Speeches were made, and big plans were announced, but nobody thought anybody had the solutions. It was a mess.

And then, on April 4 of the following year, Martin Luther King Jr. was assassinated in Memphis. Racial tensions were exploding all over the nation, including up in Boston, and James Brown was supposed to be in concert the next night. Boston's mayor was afraid that there could be riots coming out of the concert, but he knew if he canceled the show, that would provoke a response too. So they decided to broadcast the concert live on public television, hoping to keep most Bostonians in their homes watching TV.

Then, during the concert, things started going crazy. A black fan started moving toward the stage to dance, and a white police officer pushed him back. Things got tense quickly, until Brown stopped the music and said, "Wait a minute, wait a minute now, WAIT! Step down, now, be a gentleman . . . Now, I asked the police to step back because I think I can get some respect from my own people."

Brown defused the situation, the show went on, and Boston had peace that night—which was quite different than what happened in so many other cities. James Brown, the musician-social warrior, right?

———————

Fast-forward to December 13, 1980, and the fourth episode of *Saturday Night Live*, during my crazy and tumultuous first season being on *SNL* (right after the Belushi and Lorne Michels era). Jamie Lee Curtis was set to host the show, and someone came in and told us that James Brown would be the musical guest. I knew I wanted to meet him. But meeting him wasn't a given. I was just barely known at the time, and the music guests would often just come in, do their thing, and then leave. As James said, "You hit it, and then you quit it."

James did his sets that night, and no one ripped up NBC's Studio 8H like he did—nobody. Not Prince, not the Stones, not Aretha

Franklin. Respect to them all, but James Brown rocked that room like I've never seen since. I had chills watching this guy work. After his last set, I stalked him. He's walking offstage as we went to commercial break. I'm going around the other way to take the shortcut to the dressing rooms of that night's hosts. I get there just as the door closes behind him, leaving me on the outside. I go, "Oooh, missed my chance."

But then, crazy me, I just knock on the door anyway. It opens, and this big bodyguard stands there looking at me. He cocks his head to the side, and his face says, "What are you doing here?" Here I am, only four episodes into my new career on TV, looking up at a mass of muscles who apparently hasn't seen my work at The Improv. Or the Buick commercials. He must have missed those.

I say, "I'm a new cast member, and I idolize James. Can I see him?"

The door closes.

Ugh, I think. *I hope I didn't make a fool of myself.*

The door slowly opens again, and the guard steps away. And there's my hero, James Brown. Glistening with all his trademark James Brown sweat. He's sitting in the dressing room chair with the cape still on—the whole outfit he just performed in. James looks up at me as I walk over.

"Mr. Brown," I say, "I'm Joe Piscopo, a new cast member on the show. I've got to tell you, I'm your biggest fan, man."

James talks like he sings. Which means I can't quite understand anything he says in response, beyond the "Hey, hey." But I don't care. I don't care at all.

That's the day I became friends with James Brown.

To this day, in my basement music studio at home, I have pictures of Sinatra, Hendrix, Buddy Rich on drums—and a life-size cutout of James Brown, "The hardest working man in show business."

In that sense, I consider James a mentor from afar. You don't need to have a physical mentor, someone who actually meets with you and coaches you on what to do. You can learn by watching those who came before you or who are leading in your field in the present moment.

If you're a performer, no matter what genre you're working in, strive to be like James. Be the person others will say this about: "Nobody works harder than him."

––––––––––

People often ask me why I'm not countercultural, running down traditional values and the country, since I'm a comic and entertainer. Honestly, as much as I respect the comedians they have in mind when they make the comparison, the truth is—that's just not me.

I grew up in the same "Newark suburbs" location and graduated from high school about the same year as the fictional character Merry Levov (had she not bombed the local post office before finishing high school). She's the daughter in Philip Roth's novel *American Pastoral*, played marvelously by Dakota Fanning in the 2016 film version with Ewan McGregor and Jennifer Connelly. In real life, my grandparents lived in the same neighborhood, just blocks from where the "Swede" (and Roth) went to high school. My grandpa was even a craftsman in a hat factory, similar to how the Levovs owned a glove factory!

We—(me and the fictional Merry)—both witnessed firsthand the same 1967 riots in Newark, New Jersey. These events impacted both of us significantly—but differently. The trauma of what she saw radicalized Merry, and she responded with violence against the dominant values of American society and her parents. In contrast, my belief in the American dream did not fall apart. The green pastures of the "American pastoral" I experienced as a child and teen guided me through the not-so-still waters our nation and my community faced in my high school years. As a result, I didn't feel the need to rip apart the fabric of my youth, family, and culture.

Not every comedian who came of age in the sixties broke left, liberal, and countercultural. I came of age during this turbulent season of our nation's history, and I remained grounded. That's a narrative that doesn't get told enough, right? I made many mistakes during these years, but I also found my way out of trouble when I discovered the theater department in high school. Mostly, I just had a lot of fun with family and friends.

4

JONESING & CATATONIA DREAMING

After I received the Lincoln Center Student Arts Award, my drama mentor wanted to help me get into the acting program at New York University. He could have done it, too, even with my bad grades, because he had connections and friends in that world. Looking back, that's exactly what I should have done. But I told him, "I'm going to Jones College in Florida." Huh? What was I thinking?

My father wanted me to go to college, and I wanted to honor his influence on my life. So we went to a local college fair nearby in Paramus and then followed that up with some visits to the schools. Jones College consisted of one building right on the St. Johns River, next to the Matthews Bridge—this was before Jacksonville was a metropolitan town. But once I saw the local beaches, I knew that's where I would go because I loved surfing.

In the 1970s, people started using the word *jonesing* to describe a person who had a strong craving for something—usually a drink or drug of choice. I wasn't into drugs, but man did I love to surf. I headed to Jacksonville because I was jonesing to put my long board into the crashing waves of the Atlantic Ocean.

I could surf while in college?!? was my basic thought process. Seriously, that was the deciding factor for my eighteen-year-old self when selecting a school.

Jones would have me, so I had Jones.

———

I knew all the guys at Jones who were from the North, those of us who had made the trek to Florida from Boston, New York, and New Jersey. We were all going to stick together. But even with that, I got homesick and wanted to quit after two weeks.

My father got on the phone with me and gave me a talk: "Son, don't quit school, because if you do, you're going to go to Vietnam. And unless you go to officer training school, you're going to be first in line as a lieutenant."

Now, like I said, Pop served with valor in the Second World War—a real patriot and man of courage. There was nothing unpatriotic about him, so I had never heard my father talk like that to me. But this was the fall of 1969 and things with the war in Vietnam were unraveling, so Dad just wanted me to think carefully about the next move I made. Freshman year blues wasn't a reason to quit school.

Pop followed up that talk with a steady stream of encouragement, including a handwritten letter, which I now have framed and hanging on my home studio wall.

MEMO FROM THE DESK OF JOSEPH P PISCOPO

5/13/70

Dear Joe,

Hang in. Don't quit now. You have too much to lose. You have been through these crises before. Be

polite and gracious to everybody and you will come
out OK.

Someday you will look back and smile at what now
seems to be a serious problem.

Go to class and sweat out the last 4 weeks.

Love Dad
Joe Piscopo

———————

And thank God for Dad's letter because I stuck it out and soon fell
in love with radio. Jones College owned a 100,000-watt FM station,
WKTZ—a monster station broadcasting from Valdosta, Georgia, to
Daytona, Florida. I got a job at the station, working from 6:00 p.m.
until midnight. We played "Beautiful Music"—literally, that was the
station's branding. And I would talk at the quarter-hour breaks. Every
fifteen minutes or so I would break into the "beautiful music" and tell
the listener what they just heard: "That was Percy Faith playing 'Rain
Drops Keep Falling on My Head.'"

But the station's rules were very strict. If I cross-faded a song—
overlapping the ending of one song into the beginning of the next—I
would get yelled at by the manager.

"Piscopo! You can't cross-fade!"

They just wanted to hear the music. I wanted to do more.

Going to school in Jacksonville, Florida, meant flying, which
wasn't cheap. So that meant I came home only on the holidays. But
one year, when I was working for a different station, the local rock and
roll station WPDQ, the manager came in and made me a proposition:
"We want to put you on the air." I jumped at the chance. It was the
first Christmas I had ever missed with my family, but it was the right
thing to do for my career aspirations.

WPDQ didn't have all the rules that WKTZ did for how things had to be done. Entertain the audience: That was the only rule. So I was a disc jockey on the weekends, and I totally fell in love with it. I also worked at a classical music station and even a soul music station—an all-black music station where I was the only white guy there. But I absolutely loved the music, and that came through over the airwaves.

A turning point came when I was offered a spot on the local ABC affiliate, WJKS Channel 17. I'd be on TV! Some girls and I would serve as cohosts, doing the talking for the local station breaks during the national *Good Morning America* program. How great would that be? But I turned it down because I didn't want to get stuck. I knew a lot of people who came to Florida for one reason or another and always talked about making it in New York or New Jersey, but they never got out of Florida—they never came back to the city. I knew that if I stayed for that job in Florida, I never would leave. So I turned the job down and came back to Jersey.

When I look back on how I went to Jacksonville and Jones for surfing and a good time, I have to thank God for letting me take that path. I took a degree in broadcast management; though I always wanted to be the guy sitting behind the microphone—not the boss who ran the outfit. All that to say, my vocational roots aren't actually in comedy but in live radio and entertainment. Which means I've come full circle because I'm on the radio six days a week: twenty hours of live talk radio on one of the biggest stations in NYC, plus a three-hour Frank Sinatra music program on Sunday nights. The job I have now is the same job I started out doing in college—and I love it. How many people can say that?

It's amazing how God had a way of making something out of an eighteen-year-old's desire to surf.

Catatonia

While in college, I fell in love with Nancy Jones, and we got married in December 1973. Nancy and I moved back up to Jersey from

Florida, and I went into a catatonic stupor for about the next two years. We were living outside of Princeton and having a nice little life together, except I just remember waking up not sure where I was headed in life. What I was going to do. Nancy supported us mostly, working as a legal secretary, while I took odd jobs. I was a moving man. I did maintenance at a gym. No real plan or purpose. Just working at whatever I found.

Don't believe anyone who tells you that life is a straight and smooth path—it's not. I didn't know if I had what it took to make it. Hell, I didn't even know what I was trying to "make it" in. When I talk to young people today, I hear the same thing a lot (no matter how they posture themselves on social media). If you're like that and don't feel like you've got everything figured out yet, hang in there. After all, the wilderness years come before the promised land, right?

A little radio station in Trenton, New Jersey, posted a job offering, and I took it: seven days a week for $160. I did an eight-hour shift on Saturdays.

As I kept grinding away month after month in radio, I realized I was comfortable talking live to the unseen audience, cutting up and having a good time. I kept thinking about the live comedy that was all the rage. It seemed fun—maybe I should try it. So I said to Nancy and to myself, "Before I make a plan to do something else with my life—something normal—I want to try this comedy thing out."

The Support I Needed When I Needed It

At some point I told my parents, "I'm going to be a comedian."

Imagine that conversation: Your father's an influential lawyer. Your uncles are engineers. And you're going to be a what? A comedian? That's what you could expect any parent to say, right?

But Pop never questioned it at all. I think that's amazing because I know so many of us who came up in the 1960s and 1970s did things in ways that challenged and scared our Greatest Generation parents. We Baby Boomers had new ways of living and thinking, and often our parents pushed back hard. "What? That's no way to make a living!"

But not Pop. Not once. Not one time. He said, "Look, whatever you do, make sure you work hard and do it to the best of your talents." He was very supportive, even though I didn't do what he had maybe hoped I would do: go to law school. My father knew that your intellect has to be so acute to understand law like that, and I just wasn't a student.

"Pop," I said, "I can't go to law school."

And he was fine with it. My father said to me, "Look, son, if you want to go into entertainment, you know who your role model should be? Frank Sinatra. He was the greatest in the world, and he really reached the height of everything in entertainment. There's your role model. You watch Frank, son."

Pop and Sinatra were the same exact age and were both North Jersey Italian Americans. Plus, I think my father could have been a great actor and writer, and he saw himself—and me—that way. So he really began to dig the idea as I got started.

Mom, however, wasn't so keen on the idea. She looked at me with love and tiny bit of "ugh" on her face. "No, you should go to grad school," I remember her saying. "You should go get more education." She was practical and wanted me to study more—like Dad and his brother had done. I really kind of regret all the trouble I gave her in school because I never took it seriously. She said, "You have to study. You have to study."

But I remember saying to her, "Mom. Even if I've got to sleep in the gutter, I want to see if I can do this."

So many people tell stories about "I did dinner theater once and everyone loved my act." Or they recall how in high school they excelled in the leading roles in the theater productions. Others took notice and encouraged them to go further. They got busy with other things, good things perhaps—life and love and family. But here they are, middle-aged and living out the lyrics of Bruce Springsteen's "Glory Days."

Springsteen released that song a decade after my conversation with Mom, but it resonates with what I told her that day. I didn't know for sure if I had what it took to catch a break in the business, but I knew I had to give it a shot. I didn't want to be old one day, looking back at photos of my dinner theater days and wondering where I might have gone in big-time show business had I only tried.

So I said, "Ma, let me just give it a shot. I want to play rock and roll. I want to try my hand at comedy." My mother was the rock of the family to the day she passed away (while I wrote this book). We all like to tell our dads, "You're the head of the family," but it's really the moms. I know Mom wasn't crazy about my plans, and I never aimed to be star or anything like that. All I wanted to do was to have steady work. And by the grace of God almighty, I've always been able to keep working. So Mom's happy.

Mom loved me enough to encourage me. She echoed Pop, and together they told me to go for it. I had all that beautiful family support, and for that, I know I'm a lucky one. Because without it, who knows how long I would have lasted in those early days. Without family encouragement, who wants to go onstage like that night after night?

———

In an alternate history of my life, if I hadn't made it in entertainment, then what would I have done? Given all the work I had done in local radio and TV and the fact that I earned my undergraduate degree in broadcasting, I think I would have made a career in that field—perhaps running a station or being one of the on-air voices.

But as it turned out, when I took aim at the comedy clubs of NYC—doing so in the spirit of Sinatra's "If I can make it there, I'm gonna make it anywhere"—I found my path into a career as an entertainer.

Some people will say, "You should have been a really big star."

I take that as some sort of compliment, I guess. But I am what I always wanted to be: a Blue Collar, sweat on stage, mega-hours-on-the-radio, journeyman.

The only reason, in my heart, why I wouldn't mind being on the A-List (right now, in Hollywood, I'm not even on the Wait List!), is if it helped me to help others to a greater degree than I am able to do now. But it won't keep me from trying!

By the way, my dear Mom—out of all the things I have done— loved me on the radio the best. She would listen intently every single day to every single word. She would tell me (and her friends and family) how proud she was of me on the radio. Frankly, that's all that matters.

Part 2

IF YOU CAN MAKE
IT THERE, YOU'LL
MAKE IT ANYWHERE

1976–1980

5

A STAND-UP GUY

On a bitterly freezing Monday night in February 1976, I got into my 1972 Oldsmobile Cutlass and pulled away from my home in New Jersey. I passed through the Lincoln Tunnel into New York City and traveled down West 44th Street. My destination: The Improv Comedy Club.

I had put together five minutes of some (god-awful) comedic material, and I was determined to see if I could do this and launch a career. As I approached the club, I swear, there must have been two or three hundred people all lined up hoping for a chance to do what I was hoping to do. When I saw that line of people, I just turned the corner and headed back to Jersey. I said, "No way. No way can I do this."

———

Stand-up comedy in the mid-to-late 1970s channeled the same energy that rock and roll had in the 1950s and 1960s. Everyone wanted either to be a comic or to see them perform live. Steve Martin sold out theaters and stadiums from coast to coast. *Saturday Night Live* launched in October 1975 with John Belushi, Dan Aykroyd, and Chevy Chase, quickly becoming "must-watch TV" for the younger generation. Record companies produced comedic albums that sold millions of copies. ABC transformed Robin Wiliams—a veteran at The Improv and NYC clubs—into an alien for the hilarious *Mork and Mindy*. And nearly the entire cast of the hit show *Taxi* came from a background in stand-up comedy.

Budd Friedman founded The Improv in NYC in 1963, which some describe as the first comedy club of its type in the country. By the time I came on the scene at The Improv, Friedman had moved to Los Angeles where he opened a second Improv club, which became very influential in developing talented comics who are now household names. Friedman left the New York club in the hands of his wife, Silver, and managers Judy Orbach and Chris Albrecht.

While I was working the dinner theater circuit and deejaying on local radio in New Jersey, I began to take note of all these people getting their start at The Improv and other clubs, and I thought that was a path I could take too. David Brenner's start came in 1969 at the original Improv in New York, and by the time I really took notice of him in 1974, he was a national name. Robert Klein, Richard Lewis, Billy Crystal, Freddie Prinze, Richard Belzer: All these guys broke out as stand-up comedians in New York City during those years. I thought, *Why not me?*

By the end of the 1980s, the idea of a comedy club or stand-up comedy had gone mainstream. Every city seemed to have a club, and cable TV offered programs with nothing more than recordings of stand-up comedians doing their thing at these clubs. But even in 1976 when I got my start, you could already see the future of comedy by taking a look at all the comedic talent coming to life in these places. Newspapers even began covering the comedy clubs as a regular beat. There was so much energy. I'm not the first to describe the 1970s comedy scene as the decade when comedy became like rock and roll.

So, after chickening out the first time, I went across the river to audition the next week, and I told myself the truth, "OK, now if I'm going to do this—I've got to get up my courage and do it. Because if I don't try, it will gnaw at me forever."

What I hadn't known the first week was that you had to get in line to get a number from the now-legendary Judy Orbach. They didn't give out the numbers until 8:30 p.m., but I'd talked to some people beforehand, and they told me to get there at noon. So I got there at the stroke of noon for an 8:30 audition.

The numbers Judy handed out were the order in which you would go up onstage. But you didn't want to be first, because it's too fresh of an audience. Instead, you wanted to be third or fourth. We'd jockey for the numbers among ourselves: "I'll take number one this week. I'll do the first set, but next week I'm going later."

I remember it was freezing—the wind whipping off the Hudson River and just exploding us with cold. I would wait in my car with the heater on and then get out when it was time. And since I was the only guy with a car, many other guys sat in there with me. I can remember each of them even now, though *you* wouldn't know many of them because they never broke out. Others who did go on to fame—like Larry David and Alan Colmes—waited in line like the rest of us because we were all new and unknown.

Everybody was working hard, hoping to catch a break and make it there or anywhere. Even if you waited in your car, everyone could see who got there first. I would be there with Gilbert Gottfried and Alan Colmes. We'd wait eight and a half hours and fight for that number—and for what? To get inside and do our five minutes of material at 9:30 or 10:00 at night. With no compensation, of course.

We'd wait for the show to start, about 9:00 p.m. We'd sit at the bar and wait for our turn. Lots of waiting.

And then, you'd hear your name: "OK. Joe Piscopo. Piscopo, you're up. You're up, Joe."

Oh man, that was like an adrenaline rush to hear your name called.

Guys like Robin Williams and Rodney Dangerfield could take as long as they wanted, of course, as they killed the room with their acts.

But we nobodies had just five minutes. There was this light at the end of the entrance where you came in. And they'd blink that thing to let you know your time was through.

People ask, "How did the managers know if you were any good?" The answer, pure and simple: audience laughter. That's it. Immediate feedback of approval or rejection.

If you're an aspiring singer, your feedback is the level of applause at the very end of your song. But stand-up is a second-by-second affirmation or rejection. Every few seconds another opportunity for a laugh (or not) was out of your mouth and into their ears. And after waiting eight hours in the cold, that five minutes of material would be over so quick it would make your head spin.

Why only five minutes? That's a question only non-comedians ask because anyone who has tried to be a comic knows that it takes hours and hours of work to come up with even five minutes of good material.

I'm an old-fashioned guy with old-fashioned values. But when I started out, we would go into the gutter. We would use foul language. This flowed downstream from Lenny Bruce. We all figured, "Hey, Lenny Bruce can do it. We can do it, right?" But then people would say, "Joe, you don't need it. It's not you." So to this day, I'm very clean onstage.

That's where Eddie Murphy and I differed a bit back then. I would ask him, "Why are you using vulgar language onstage?" and he'd say, "Because they're laughing." Now, I didn't have an argument against him on that point because he was funny when did it. He used profanity, and it was hysterical. But it can be a crutch for comedians trying to catch a break. I know that when I started out, it was a crutch. You droped an "f-bomb"—and it seemed to help. But I think now that if the vulgar accentuates the joke, maybe the joke isn't worthy.

Look at Jerry Seinfeld. Not an inappropriate word out of his mouth, and yet he's funnier than anybody. Jerry says that he used to swear in his early stand-up, but stopped because he decided it was the cheap way to get the laugh. He realized, "That's the only reason they laughed at that. It's just you didn't find the gold."[10]

I like that: "You didn't find the gold." I think that's good advice to young comics and entertainers. In your prep, find the gold. Don't just go after the easy laugh. Work hard to develop your unique God-given gold.

So, call me what you like, but I like it clean and character-driven. You don't have to lean on any of that shock value. Just give it to me funny.

My comedy was mostly observational material, for lack of a better way of saying it. I would read the headlines—the current events everyone was talking about—and I'd just think of what I hoped was a funny take on these news stories.

For example, when Ronald Reagan was running for president in 1979, Iran had taken all those American hostages. In the months leading up to the election, news analysts all talked about what kind of mental calculations the terrorists were making when they looked at Jimmy Carter versus Ronald Reagan. Iran held them in captivity for 444 days, releasing them within the hour after Reagan's inauguration. I remember getting up at The Improv and doing a bit about Reagan, complete with a Middle Eastern accent: "Holy moly. This guy Reagan is crazy, man. We better let these guys go." Stuff like that—political news and local New York hot topics.

I'd rather do a performance piece that was accurate and spot-on. More of an acting piece. I felt more comfortable doing that. You know, if you have the gift of Jerry Seinfeld, of Bill Cosby, of Lewis Black, these instinctively brilliant comic minds, then you go that route! But you gotta know your limitations.

Here's my confession: I was never a comic. I'm not a comedian. I was, and am, an entertainer. I always just wanted to work as a journeyman.

You've got to know what your strengths are and use what God gave you. No matter what your job is, that's the way to be: authentic to yourself. Sure, you can make improvements and practice lifelong learning—always getting better. But like I tell young people, and my own kids: The key to your life's work will be determined by how you develop the skills you're naturally good at, you enjoy doing, and that there's a market for. Don't fight it. And that's why I've always said and continue to say: I'm an entertainer with over five decades of work— but I'm not a comedian.

———

After several weeks seeing my comic bits and my banter with the audience, The Improv manager, Chris Albrecht, took a liking to me. We called him "the General" because he had a whole litany of comics that he oversaw. Chris could get down with the guys. We played softball, we'd play baseball, we'd go to ball games, and we would do guy things. But he was always kind of the boss.

One Saturday night, at two in the morning, we still had a full house. Albrecht said, "Piscopo, you're up next. Get up on the mic. Follow me."

I thought, *Oh, man. This is the check spot. Two o'clock.*

The "check spot" means that all the checks went out for the food and beverages the patrons had consumed during the show. It's the worst time for any performer because when you see a large bill, you get irritable, and nobody is funny for a few minutes until you forget about the check and relax again. So no comedian wants to be in the check spot.

But I'm still auditioning to become a regular, so I go up onstage and start my bit—telling my jokes. But I'm not really clicking. At least not until someone in the audience starts to heckle me a little bit. I respond in like manner, dishing it back at the man: "Oh, is that right, pal? What do you do for a living?"

I talk to the guy back and forth, and I was super quick on my feet, something like, "What career are you in that you can wear an outfit like that in public and make fun of me?" Boom. That sort of thing. I was like a young version of Don Rickles, the late, great genius of razor-sharp-insult comedy.

Another guy heckles me and—boom!—I respond back. Not with jokes but with quick wit that got the audience laughing. Five minutes turn into fifteen before they let me off that stage.

As I walk off the stage and make my way back to the bar, I look over at Albrecht. He would sit in the back of the club and watch the comedians from his doorway, like a Roman emperor in the Coliseum dispensing approval or disapproval with just a look or a wave of the hand. He looks at me and points, motioning for me to come to him. I'm going, "Oh man. Maybe I did something wrong."

So I walk over and Chris says, "All right. You proved yourself, Joe. You're a regular. You're going to be a regular now."

That was like being knighted. You're a regular. Wow! You never forget those moments of success in your career, especially the early triumphs.

Being a regular worked out for the best for me because I always felt most comfortable improvising onstage, just coming up with funny things on the spot. Albrecht turned me into the master of ceremonies, introducing people on the stage. And for me, that's when the fun started, as I got to bring out laughter from the audience alongside all these great performers: Robin Williams, Andy Kaufman, Jerry Seinfeld, Rodney Dangerfield—the list just goes on and on of all the comedians who came through the door at The Improv.

Albrecht went on to become my agent and then a legendary TV executive, developing hit shows like *The Sopranos* and *Sex in the City*. But for me, everything began at Improv. Albrecht was the General, and with that finger he kept my young dreams alive.

———

People ask me what it was like to be on the stage at The Improv when I was new, untested, and unknown. What did I see when I looked out from the stage? How did I feel? What was going through my mind?

Well, first of all, you're just overwhelmed with fear. You have a dark, dark room with sometimes just twenty people in it—if you got called up really late. But then, you'd sometimes get onstage with a full packed house—every eye on you—and there must have been several hundred people at those times. You'd stand in front of this brick wall with just the microphone in front of you. Off to the side was a really old, out of tune upright piano.

You'd be trying your best to run through your material, moving from one bit to the next. Your eyes were always on that light at the back that would blink if you went over your five- or seven-minute set, because you never wanted to bump into the next comic's time.

It really is the best training ground, but it comes loaded with fear too. When you step onstage, you've got to feel it. Fear at first, and after a while you realize that's your comfort zone. And it's like kind of an affliction, actually—that desire to get onstage. Even to this day, if I step onstage and all eyes are on me, I feel that same "do or die" emotion that comes with performing live. There's no safety net. There are no second takes.

By the grace of God, it's just a comfort zone that I enjoyed after a while, though at first when I heard, "Here's Joe Piscopo, a new comic you're going to love"—I won't lie to you—that was frightening. There was always competition in the air—mostly positive but sometimes toxic. And talent scouts would be in the audience looking for fresh faces for TV talk shows. But perhaps nothing would ratchet up the nerves more than when you'd look out into the audience and see big-name celebrities there to see the show. Or famous comedians would just show up unannounced in order to get up onstage and try out some new material they were working on—usually in preparation for being a guest on Johnny Carson's *The Tonight Show*.

By the time I got to The Improv, Bette Midler, who had performed there regularly when she was getting her start, was already a major star. But she'd still come into the club from time to time, and we'd perform for her. She was very quiet, and she'd sit way in the back. I remember how we no-name newbies would get onstage together, and I'd play the piano (thanks, Mom, for those lessons!)—and we'd all sing and goof around for laughs. Midler seemed to enjoy this, though she probably doesn't even remember it now. When you're young and hoping to make it in entertainment, getting a smile or laughs from someone who's already established is a boost of confidence to fragile egos.

I've always wished that I could have calmed down and appreciated the comedy clubs more—and my time doing *Saturday Night Live* too (but I'll save that for later). I look back and think, *What the freak, man, that was fun! What was I thinking about?* But you're just scared too much when you're new.

———

Standing onstage in front of strangers to make them laugh can be daunting, like being asked to take your clothes off in a public place—not that I've had that happen to me.

But there was one memorable night. I'm sitting there at the bar at The Improv, and this young drunk guy, a customer, starts belting out a Paul McCartney song. Now, I'm new and don't know what to expect, so I'm mildly amused as he sings. But then it gets weird.

At the end of each line of lyric, the guy starts to take his clothes off. He sings, "Someone's knocking at the door" . . . and off go his shoes. "Someone's ringing the bell" . . . off come the pants.

Each line of the song goes by quicker than you can imagine, and now the guy is standing there, right in the middle of the tables and chairs—butt naked.

I'm a kid from Jersey just trying to break into comedy, now with partial responsibilities to emcee and be a doorman. And I have no idea what to do.

Albrecht comes up to the guy and very gingerly takes his arms from behind and leads him to the door, opens it up, and tosses him outside, into the snow—during a blizzard.

So he's walking down the street butt naked—still singing, "Someone's knocking at the door"—when Judy Orbach feels sorry for him. She grabs his clothes and belongings and runs out the door with some others in order to find the guy. This is late at night in Hell's Kitchen in 1976, so what happens next is inevitable: They get robbed on the way to return the pants to the drunk McCartney wannabe. The robber doesn't just take the guy's wallet—he takes the pants and underwear too.

Ain't that crazy? Shows you how tough New York was at the time and the rock-and-roll atmosphere of The Improv.

If you've never been to a comedy club—or never been to one that was set up like The Improv—you might have the wrong idea about its ambiance and atmosphere. The Improv wasn't like walking into a symphony hall or concert arena where everyone has theater seating and is expected to keep quiet during the performance.

The Improv served food and beverages, which were the main money makers, the way the lights were kept on—not the admission ticket. The music and comedy provided the entertainment for the patrons, but they weren't sitting still and quiet. Not at all.

So in addition to the nerves you're already feeling—*Can I hold their attention? Will they think I'm funny?*—you also have to compete for the audience's attention with waitresses walking around taking orders from the menu and with the sounds of clinking glasses and silverware against dishes. If you listen to Frank Sinatra's *Sands* album, you will hear that—the clinks of glasses and coffee cups being put down on the tables.

You're standing right at the front in front of the brick wall. Then there are two rows of tables, one on the left, one on the right. And an aisle for the waitress in the middle, on the right side. To the left side, there's a patron sitting virtually on the stage. And then there were tables in booths and more tables after that. And there was a whole back area, which is where the celebrities often gathered. The Improv probably put out more tables and chairs than they were allowed. So many people could pack in there, and they're all staring at you up on that tiny stage. But you could really only see the people in the first couple of rows because of the spotlight. The rest of it is always relatively dark.

My job as emcee and doorman was to wrangle the crowd and make them feel comfortable. Being respectful to them, I'd settle the crowd down and make sure we had all their focus before we would bring on a comic like Dangerfield or Robin Williams up to the stage.

We'd do two or three shows a night. There would be a line outside the door waiting to get in. One show would end, and we'd reset, then open the doors again for the next show. Jam packed. Get them in, get them out. I think the owners did very well there. I know that we barely got any money. We got "cab fare," meaning that we'd get maybe twenty or thirty bucks per show, just enough for a cab ride home. If you did three sets a night, you might make a hundred bucks or so.

Physically, the place was dank, dark, and dirty. But it was riveting—absolutely a driving force and an energy that I feel lucky to have been a part of. Like I said, it was like rock and roll. Everybody wanted to see who was going to be the next to breakout in comedy. I think a movie or a Netflix series should be made about this slice of pop culture and comic history.

I don't know who to credit for it turning so energetic—why it started when it did. Andy Kaufman? Robin Williams? Or even earlier: Woody Allen, Robert Klein, Richard Pryor? But it was like the birth of a whole different entertainment—live comedy, man. And the customers walked in the door to discover who was going to be the next hot commodity comedian.

Catch a Rising Star—Literally

There were three main comedy clubs in New York: The Improv, Catch a Rising Star, and Comic Strip. The Improv was my club. Like most guys back then, I kind of jockeyed back and forth between clubs, but I was definitely more of an Improv guy because I was also the emcee and the doorman.

One day, Rick Newman at Catch a Rising Star called, "I really want you to emcee on Sunday night at Catch. Belzer can't make it, so I want you to cover for him."

Richard Belzer was one of the great stand-ups in New York at the time. He never had material, but he worked with the crowd brilliantly. The Belz—he was the guy. He was older than me by a few years and had been doing this scene longer.

I was like, "Wow—sure, I'll go." What a break I was getting. And boy, oh boy—did I ever get broken that night.

So I went down to 78th on 1st Avenue and showed up, wide-eyed and all.

George Wallace, one of the great comedians of our time, was there with a few others who were all doing the Sunday night set. It was a nice crowd, and everything was going good. I'd stand up and say a few things, intro the next act, and interact with the crowd. What could go wrong?

There was a real quiet group in the back of the joint, all very well dressed. And they all had "painted ladies"—beautiful women done up with makeup and hair and fancy outfits. It was straight out of the Copacabana scenes in *Goodfellas*, though that movie came out fifteen years later.

I'm up onstage interacting with the crowd, and I make the mistake of saying, "What are you guys doing in the back there? Where are you from?" Just like that.

And then . . . no response. Nothing. Nothing at all.

Being stupid and naive—and with nobody at the club making a motion to me to move on—I repeat myself. I mean, if folks just ignore you when you interact with them, it creates some tension that comic-emcees like to exploit for laughs. You're going to ignore me? I'll just double down then, right?

That's when I say these words: "What, are you in the mob or something?"

Just like that. That's actually what I say to a table full of mafiosos and their girlfriends. Each fellow with his *goomada*.

Nobody warned me that this club was controlled by the mob. I'm a comic from New Jersey, doing bits on the West Side. What did I know? Why didn't the management tell the new guy, me, that the club is owned by the mafia? That the mob guys come in here and that you don't interact with them. You don't talk to the people in the back. You don't point them out to the audience. And you certainly don't make fun of them. Nobody told me that this was the club where Jerry

Seinfeld had a beer stein thrown at him a few months before—by the very same guy I had just heckled. Nobody told me that Belzer had once been thrown down the stairs of the basement. Yep, it was mob-owned and there were a bunch of wise guys there.

And so, this guy comes over to me. "Hey, you know, we don't appreciate you making fun of us."

I say, "I'm sorry, sir. We're just kidding around. I hope you don't mind."

Then, the manager of the place does the dumbest thing possible. He says, "Why don't you take this outside?"

So this guy makes a move to take my elbow and walk me outside.

"Whoa, wait a minute," I respond and then start walking away—or trying to.

Forget about getting away. These guys take the name of the club literally: Catch a Rising Star. As soon as I step out into the lobby, they push me into the coat room and the goons jump me. Just like you see in the movies.

All of a sudden, I've got three or four guys on me. They're not in a mood to talk—though that doesn't keep me from trying to dialogue my way out of the dilemma.

We're tussling in the coat room, and I say, "Look, I'm sorry if you're upset."

He slaps my face.

"There's no reason to get excited," I say. "We can settle this."

Another guy slaps me in the face.

"Hey now. You don't have to get violent because if you—"

He hits me again. And this time I go after him.

So now there's a brawl. The rest of the mob guys start piling on me, and I'm just getting pummeled. They've got me bent over and they're beating the heck out of me.

I looked up at my fellow comics, sitting at the bar watching all this. One of them is George Wallace, one of the great comedians and a friend of mine. Now, he's like seven feet tall and huge. To this day we joke about what happened that night, because when I looked up at him for help, I could see in his eyes what he was thinking in his brain: *Oh good! I'm going to get Joe's spot tonight.*

As I'm getting turned into pulp, my buddy John DeBellis, God bless him, says three of the most important words I need to hear at this moment: "Run, Joe, run!"

The muscles are grabbing me all over, and at some point, they latch onto my sweater. I slide out of it somehow, leave it behind with them, and take off running down 1st Avenue as fast as I can. I was real quick back in the day.

The other comedians came out the door and caught up with me. Everyone insisted I go to Lenox Hill Hospital nearby. I almost refused, but in the end I'm glad I went because that guy had beaten the hell out of me. I had a black eye, a broken nose, and a chipped tooth. In less than a minute, he had hit me real hard at least three times in that small space. He was a professional, and he was concise.

I later found out his name was "Johnny Rip" or something like that, and that he eventually went up the river. Bill Maher, who got his start at Catch a Rising Star, once said, "We all remember the night they kicked the shit out of Joe Piscopo."[11] Thanks, Bill.

Seinfeld wrote about his own experience getting a beer stein thrown at him by "Rip," and added,

> A few months later, Joe Piscopo dealt with the same guy from the "Catch" stage. The thug grabbed Joe and broke his nose. A few hours later Joe returned from the hospital with his face all bandaged up only to find this mobster still sitting in his seat enjoying the show. I guess once you pay the cover price no matter what you do you never have to leave.
>
> I went on to have a TV show. Joe starred on *Saturday Night Live*. Obviously, this guy had an eye for talent.[12]

You gotta love how Jerry can observe *anything* and turn the event into comedic gold.

Anyhow, my father wrote a lawyerly letter to the attorney representing these guys. Now, you've got to understand something about my dad. His legal colleagues nicknamed him "Poison Pen Piscopo" because he was so eloquent and incisive in his writing prowess. He could have been a writer; he was so smart and so gifted with words.

So, Pop wrote this letter, and then we followed it up by going to this other lawyer's office. We sat down across the desk. He looked us up and down and then said, "We've got $10,000 we could offer you" (about $50,000 today).

My father took a look at this man and knew exactly what we were really dealing with. He knew we weren't going to get more than that and that it would be dangerous to press the issue further. He told the lawyer, "Fine. Yes, OK. We agree to your offer."

We took the money and got the hell out of there.

———

Speaking of hell, The Improv isn't in Hell's Kitchen anymore—it's now in the fashionably called "Clinton Hill." And crime may not be way down, but property values are up. When you watch Robert De Niro in his Oscar-winning performance in *Taxi Driver*, keep in mind that the picture was mostly set and filmed in Hell's Kitchen. *Taxi Driver* released the same month I started out at The Improv, so if you want a picture of the neighborhood I worked in the evening and early morning hours, watch the movie and take note of all the darkness, grime and crime, despondency, and death. There's a reason Martin Scorsese chose to film the movie in Hell's Kitchen.

The Improv's building remains, of course, but now it's a swanky restaurant called Don Giovanni. There's been an unbelievable turnaround in the neighborhood from when we were doing stand-up there. I mean, they didn't drop the neighborhood's name—Hell's

Kitchen—but now people sit outside and eat fantastic Italian food. This was a hellhole during my days at The Improv, with drug dealers and prostitutes and crime everywhere—just an awful place. There was a deli called Smilers just across the street from The Improv (which is still there by the way). But if we wanted to go to Smilers, then we'd make sure to walk with someone else. I'd grab Larry David: "Larry, walk with me, will you? I'm going to Smilers." You couldn't walk by yourself without getting mugged—and even with two guys you might not be safe.

What an era. What a way to be brought up in the business—doing four and a half years of comedy and entertainment at The Improv. That's how I came to discover that my best work flowed out of me during live performances. There's nothing like doing live entertainment—I live for live. Even today, I do stage entertainment constantly, and twenty-three hours of live radio every single week—and a steady stream of live TV news segments too. This is my comfort zone. I can be as nervous as anything, right before I get onstage or in the radio studio, but once the show is on, I'm more comfortable there than anywhere else in life. And I think that is either a disease or it's just something innate in your chemical makeup as a person. You're either there or you're not. And apparently, I'm there, because I'm still in the radio booth all week and on the road every weekend.

One more thing about doing The Improv: It was a great showcase for me because that's how I ended up getting jobs—first doing commercials and then *Saturday Night Live*. Both of those came to me because of the bits and the emceeing I was doing every night.

Of course, no man is an island, and no success I've experienced ever came in a vacuum. I had support from friends.

6

WITH A LITTLE HELP FROM MY FRIENDS

If you drive into Manhattan every night to emcee to unruly crowds all the way to three in the morning, you quickly realize just how much you need to find genuine friends, mentors, and generous spirits. To this day, I'm friends with all the guys I spent months or years with at The Improv. Was there spirited competition and rivalry between us? Yes, of course. We all wanted the same thing: to keep on working until we broke out and made a career of this. But there was also friendship and camaraderie. We were in it together. Out of the thousands and thousands of people who showed up for an audition, only a few dozen survived the cuts or lasted more than a year.

We were the few—the happy few. We were a band of brothers.

Mentors and Generous Spirits

When I use that term *mentor* I don't mean to imply there was any *formal* mentorship. That's not the way things work in comedy clubs.

You just sit back and observe the veterans of entertainment—onstage and off. You take notes of how they develop their material, how they perform, how they handle applause and heckling, how they handle themselves offstage. These kinds of things are "caught, not taught" as the old saying goes.

Sometimes you just got lucky and met comedians and entertainers who were generous spirits, giving of themselves to you and doing so when nobody was looking.

One night in early 1976—right as I was getting started—I sat at the bar waiting to go onstage at Catch a Rising Star. This guy walks in and comes over to where I am standing.

"Hey, how you doing?" I said.

He says, "Good. How you doing?"

"What's your name?" I ask.

"John Belushi," he says, and points to another guy with him. "This is my friend, Danny Aykroyd."

"Hi fellas," I said. "Are you going onstage?"

"Nah, we're just here to watch," Belushi says. "We're doing this new show in town."

"What's the show?" I ask with all sincerity and naivety.

"*Saturday Night Live.*"

"Cool. Oh, that's cool."

I had no idea. I worked every Saturday night in the clubs and had never caught the show, which was only a few months old at the time. And of course, this was long before the internet. I just didn't know much if anything about *SNL*—and I didn't know Belushi or Aykroyd yet. I could never have predicted that five years later I would be on that show, to replace the original cast who by then had become comic and TV legends.

That night at the bar, I just sat talking with these two fellows who didn't put on airs, didn't try to tell me how important they were, and treated me as if I was already a full member of the same guild they were. That's having a generosity of spirit. I'll say more about Belushi and Aykroyd on this point later in the book.

Danny Aiello, a veteran of The Improv, was one of my dearest friends—though we didn't work at The Improv at the same time. But later on, when I was getting started, he'd come back in as a customer, and I was always in awe. It was the same thing with Robert Klein. I'd be like, "Wow, these guys both came out of The Improv and look where they are now." They were mentors to me from afar as I watched how they did their work.

———————

Robin Williams was one of the most giving performers I ever met. It's fascinating how someone as brilliant as he was would be that generous. What I mean is he would go up onstage with his rapid-fire delivery and would get laugh after laugh after laugh. He would just build it up. Boom. Boom. Boom. The audience would be gasping for breath from laughter. And then, he would take a step back, look over at you—the next guy, the one who would have to follow him—and that was your opening to go up and start. He would just hand the happy audience right off to you and give you all this audience energy he had created. You never forget that kind of thing, that bigness of heart and generosity.

Not all the big stars were like that with the unknown guys who were struggling to make it. I don't want to mention names because I'm not that kind of person. But I've worked with people who would hog the stage. There's just no rhythm there. When you're up onstage or doing the emceeing, your job is to make sure that the audience walks out with their friends all saying, "Did you see that?" and "That was amazing!" You want the audience to say that, and if it requires you to give the laughs to somebody else, then you do it. It's your job to make the show great. You are a team member. That's the difference between being part of an ensemble (like *Saturday Night Live*) compared to just doing your thing all by yourself.

At The Improv, there was an exit door—a fire exit just to the right of the stage. I'd be at the mic introducing people, and all of a sudden, there would be a knock on that door. I sincerely wouldn't know who was knocking, but I'd roll with it and direct the audience's attention to it.

"Let's see who's at the door," I'd say, as I walked over with the microphone. When I cracked open the door, in bounced Robin Williams.

The place would go nuts. I mean, they paid to get in and they paid to have some drinks and some food. And they knew they'd get some laughs courtesy of guys and gals like me—some who would go on to become famous performers and others who would never make it. But then, unexpectedly . . . there's Robin Williams! Unexpected and ready to give the audience twenty or thirty minutes of the best comedy. It was electric.

———————

I remember one night when I was emceeing in New York, Rodney Dangerfield came into The Improv unannounced. You're a kid and you're regularly seeing Rodney on *The Tonight Show*, and you're going like, "Wow, this is unbelievable."

In real life he was exactly what you saw on TV. It was, "Hey, how are you, how you doing? Good to see you." It was Rodney.

And then Albrecht said, "Joe, you got to bring up Rodney."

So there I was onstage—the young guy introducing the great. I got to tell you something, this is where you learn as a kid. I said, "Rodney, come on up here."

And he doesn't come up.

So I killed some time. Then I said, "Now . . . please welcome Rodney Dangerfield."

He came up. "Hey, how are you?" He does his set.

Afterward, he comes over and he goes, "Joe, you're a good kid. I like you. But you can't just say, 'Come up here,' like that. That's not very respectful."

I said, "Rodney, I'm so sorry. I had no idea."

I learned from the great Dangerfield that you intro a guest—whether they're famous or not—with respect and generosity. You'll hear me say on the radio the kind of intro I learned from Rodney: "It's very kind of you to join us. Thank you for being with us." And to the audience, "Would you please welcome . . ." and "Ladies and gentlemen, we're very privileged to have this person with us. Please give a nice round of applause for so and so."

Rodney taught me that. He was a scientist when it came to comedy, and he was probably the purest comic I know. He'd pull up in front of the club in this old Buick Electra. It was like a Cheech and Chong movie with all the weed smoke coming out. Then he'd come in and come on. He would come into The Improv and work on his material. He would formulate his *Tonight Show* set there at the clubs, six weeks ahead of when he was supposed to go on. He would add jokes, cut jokes, reword jokes. We'd write a joke for him, and if he liked it, he'd give us fifty bucks.

———

One day when I was working at The Improv and living in Tenafly, New Jersey, I stopped off at the grocery store. My son Joey, my first-born, was just a baby, and I had to pick up diapers or something. There I am in line at Grand Union—a grocery store chain that's out of business now—and while I'm paying for my stuff, the conveyer belt is rolling, and the next person's stuff is coming down the line.

Here comes a package of mozzarella cheese. And then another mozzarella. And another mozzarella. And another mozzarella.

Who needs all this mozzarella? I'm thinking.

I look up. It was Paul Sorvino.

Sorvino was one of the great actors of our time. When I was in college I saw him in *Day of the Dolphin* with George C. Scott. Let me tell you, if you're from New Jersey, when a fellow Italian hits the screen, the entire Italian community notices. It was just like that. You knew who the Italians in the movies were, and you respected them for their work.

So I looked up and said, "Mr. Sorvino, I can't believe you're here. What an honor to meet you."

"Hey, how you doing, kid?" he said.

I told him I was doing work at The Improv. He couldn't have been nicer, showing interest in what I was telling him and all.

I never forgot that. A big movie star, buying mozzarella, but taking time to show interest to some young entertainer with diapers and milk in his hands and a cheesy smile on his face.

Over the years we would appear at many of the same fundraisers and Italian American events. And years later we even did a movie together called *How Sweet It Is*.

Kindness costs so little—next to nothing, really. Sorvino gave me some that day—fifty years ago—and I'll never forget it.

At Home and at Home Plate

Me and Gilly—Gilbert Gottfried—were together as friends even before we both joined *Saturday Night Live* in 1980. We met at The Improv. He was one of the gang, right there from day one with me, and we really hit it off.

Here's this guy from the Lower East Side. A New Yorker through and through. Politically incorrect as you can get, but the sweetest, funniest guy in the world. I'd joke with him that he was helpless in many ways. At the time, he lived with his mom in an apartment and slept on the couch. He was as New York as it gets and brilliant onstage—in the vein of Robin Williams—where you can't quite keep up with the thought process, and your jaw drops at the brilliance.

I would bring Gilly onstage with me at 2:00 a.m. at The Improv as we got our start. Remember what I said in the last chapter—I was vulgar in the very beginning as I tried to find my voice. Well, Gilly was too. By today's standards, Gill and I were both politically incorrect in our jokes; I thank God there were no cell phones with cameras back then.

Gilly created a character, Murray Abramowitz—who was my manager and would always get me into these really bad deals. And that was a mantra and a thread that we always used onstage: "Look, you play The Improv. You'll go on at three o'clock in the morning! I'm gonna make you a star!" That kind of thing. Just really great fun we had, going from one club to another.

I remember once when Nancy and I were asked to house-sit. We had dear friends who lived across the street from us and our little carriage house in Englewood, New Jersey. The man was Bob Ellsworth, and he was an internationally renowned optometrist. He operated on children's eyes, a brilliant man and well known in his field. We struck up a relationship because I was a goofball for the comedy clubs, and he was this esteemed, internationally renowned medical doctor. We hit it right off.

They went on vacation and asked if we would house-sit for them.

"Sure, man. We got it."

It's a beautiful house, so what do I do? I call all my friends at The Improv, of course. What else am I going to do?

I say, "Hey, I've got a whole mansion out here, guys—come on up." And they all do. So, it's like *Home Alone* except we weren't alone.

All The Improv fellows show up—but I especially remember Gilly. He had never driven a car before. He walked everywhere or took a cab or public transit. So, I'm teaching Gilly how to drive in the big driveway of their house, but he's running over bushes. He's trying his best, but he's just awful.

And so, you've got every nut job comedian from The Improv running around the house, and we're all just having such fun. Bob was a hunter, and he had a big moose head hanging on the wall. So, of course, Gill and I start messing around with the moose, and the whole thing falls off the wall—boom! It comes crashing down. And we're trying to figure out how to get it back up on the wall, but it's not like hanging a clock, you know?

The house-sitting ended, and the Doc came back home. He never asked about the moose, so I guess we got it hung correctly, and it didn't fall again.

———————

One of the regulars at The Improv who I never ever missed a chance to watch was Larry David. When Larry went onstage, everybody stopped what they were doing and watched him do his thing. All the comics wanted to see him. And here's why: He would get into fights with the audience. "What, do you think you're funny? Do you want to try this? Do you? Do you want to try this?"

It was brilliant, absolutely brilliant. When I watch somebody, I want to be impressed. I want them to do something that I can't do. I saw Larry do a good set *one time*.

Everyone will tell you that it was obvious that Larry had the mind of a comic genius—and the fact that he went on to create both *Seinfeld* and *Curb Your Enthusiasm* is proof of this. But Larry would intentionally bomb at stand-up—all the time! He never got a laugh. He would fight with the audience. If you've seen his cantankerous persona in *Curb*, that's exactly what he was like onstage. No difference. And we would be in the back of the house going, "Oh my God, the guy's a genius. Where is he conceptually coming up with that thought process?" We would just laugh our heads off. Larry would leave the stage, and the audience would be scratching their heads: "What the hell just happened?"

————————

Most of the guys from The Improv played baseball together in Central Park on a team representing the club. We competed against all these Broadway teams, consisting mostly of the production crews and backup actors. But at least once, I played third base against Al Pacino, who was then in a Shakespearean play on Broadway. He didn't have his glove, so he asked to borrow mine each inning. I'm a Rawlings guy, but this was a Wilson Al Kaline glove. I said, "Absolutely" and gave it to him. So now, every time we're coming off the field, I have to wait to give the glove to him—which I got a kick out of because, you know, it's Al Pacino! But I knew he just wanted to unwind and play some ball, so I'd just leave my glove on third base to keep him from having to interact with a goofy fan. At least I was aware enough back then to understand that concept, right?

This was a few years after *Godfather* had made Pacino a household name but several years before I landed with *SNL*. My only movie credit at the time was three seconds as an extra on the Jeff Bridges version of *King Kong* (feel free to use that piece of trivia at your next party). I'm still trying to play it cool and not be a fanboy—but here it is, fifty years later, and I'm telling you about the day Pacino and Piscopo both played the hot corner and shared my glove. You just don't forget these memories.

The name of the team was "44th and 9th"—the location of The Improv—with the numbers printed on our shirts. We were such big baseball fans. We took it really seriously, but it was a tough league.

Actor and comedian Robert Wuhl—now famous for *Arliss*, the HBO series he created and starred in—played first base in his sports coat. I can't even explain this to you—he wore his corduroy sports coat to first base, man. I have no idea why.

Standing out in right field was our weak link defensively, my dearest friend Gilbert—not exactly an athletic specimen. Gilly had no idea what athletics meant. He was more like our mascot.

Larry David was a fantastic player—our shortstop and one of our best athletes. Larry would always be venting and complaining throughout the entire game. But one of my favorite memories was after a play where he had run down the line. I looked over at him, and he was all bent out of shape about something.

"What? What happened?" I asked.

Larry goes, "I stepped in dog doo. I can feel it."

I said, "What? Just scrape it off Larry."

A few minutes later I see Larry and he's shoeless. He's walking around in just socks. "Where's your shoes Larry?"

"I threw my shoes away," he said, still kerfuffled. "What—you think I'm going to wear them again? They've got dog shit on them."

Thirty years later, Larry's character on his hit show *Curb Your Enthusiasm* did the exact same thing—he stepped in dog poo and threw his shoes away. An example of art imitating life. You gotta love Larry David.

After the game, we'd load up in whoever owned a car, often me in my Ford Fairmont (the one Seinfeld told me looked like a government vehicle). My good friend John DeBellis would say, "Come on, my mom's making spaghetti." And we would all go—Larry, Jerry, me, Gilly—everybody would go out to John's mom's house.

So we'd play baseball together, go eat spaghetti together, and then head into The Improv together for another late night of work—which often didn't feel like work at all because of the support of friends and veterans.

Like I said, we were a band of brothers, and these were some of the best days of my life.

7

COMMERCIAL BREAKS
& BREAKING IN

Doing comedy at The Improv from 1976 to 1980 was like being in the trenches—everyone was just trying to survive and get out, to move on to the next thing, the bigger thing. Some of us did get out and went on to great things. But others—some who were very talented—we never heard from again. So it really was a wild ride.

I put in about four and a half years as the emcee at The Improv. I was the master of ceremonies and doing comedy sets and working as a character actor. I was using the stage as a means to an end, to get where I thought I wanted to go—acting in movies and TV shows. When an agent saw me onstage one night and said he wanted to represent me for commercials, I didn't know what to do. I needed more income, but I didn't know if this was the right move for the career I wanted to launch.

Best Advice I Ever Got

That's when I got the gift of brilliant advice from the husband-and-wife comic team of Anne Meara and Jerry Stiller. They came into The Improv a lot and loved to tell me their stories, mentoring and explaining how show business worked.

When the agent came in and saw the show and started pitching me to become a pitchman—an actor for TV commercials—I talked about it with the Stillers because I knew they were doing popular ads for Windex and Blue Nun Wine at the time.

"Joe, you should always do commercials—always," they said.

I asked them why.

They both looked at me with completely straight faces and said, "Because it's *F*-you money."

"*F*-you money" meant easy money you had banked doing commercials, so you could pick and choose the creative projects that came your way. You'd have enough money to do what you wanted. You could be a little more selective with what you chose to do. You could tell someone to go kiss off if they pitched you on some project you wanted no part of.

I learned that from Stiller and Meara and never forgot it. I told the agent to get me into commercials, and that's when I became a working actor.

I did funny-guy ads and straight-man pitches too.

My first TV commercial was for Hardees. We must have done fifty takes, and each time I had to take a bite of the hamburger and say "Mmmmm . . . this is good" with a big smile on my face. Of course I was smiling, they paid me $1,500 ($6,000 in today's dollars) for a few hours of pretending to eat fast food. I had to spit the food out after every take, of course, because you can't actually eat lukewarm hamburgers for three hours and not get sick. But that was my first television break.

Another of my early commercials was for Dolly Madison Ice Cream. I remember my line: "Look at all the nuts."

I did Schlitz Beer, where five guys and I acted like we were at a tailgate party having fun. Nothing like getting paid good money to drink beer in front of a camera.

Then I started scoring some of the big, national spots, like becoming the spokesman for Buick. They flew me to Detroit, and I did an entire walk-through pitch for the LeSabre. I was in a tie but had my sleeves rolled up to show I was just a regular guy. "You can get better gas mileage from this full-size Buick LeSabre than from this VW Rabbit," I said with everyman sincerity. Or these lines: "What can you get for $6,110 these days?" The answer: a Buick LeSabre. "Which, incidentally, offers an EPA estimated eighteen miles per gallon." Remember, this was 1979, so a sedan getting that kind of gas mileage was worth touting. No laughs or funny stuff—I was just there to show the value of the cars. Speaking of value, that day's work earned me $25,000 (over $100,000 in today's dollars).

But I really hit the big time when I landed with Dr. Pepper and got to work with director Bob Giraldi. He was the guy who shot all the Pepsi commercials with Michael Jackson. He shot these ads brilliantly, and he would hire me all the time. He's the reason I wound up doing all those memorable Miller Lite commercials in the 1980s.

The work that goes into making a thirty second commercial is intense because those thirty seconds are meticulous and crafted. I enjoyed doing them because they're artsy, fun, and they're quick.

I also started doing voiceovers. Everything and anything I could get my hands on to do in the business. I was working. It was great and life was good.

I started doing ads in 1977, and by 1979 I was earning $85,000 a year ($350,000 in today's dollars) from the commercials alone. That was five times greater than the median income of a household in the US in 1979. With all that money pouring in, I figured I had made it.

Yes! You Can Put Me on Hold

And that's when I started to break. NBC put me on a retainer of about $25,000 for six months at a time. This was just something they did to keep talent buttoned down—even if they don't end up using you during that time. I did the six months, and then they picked up the option for another six months.

Gilly got a retainer too, so they sent us out to LA to stand by for auditions. They put me up at the Sunset Marquis—the famous rock and roll hotel, right there off Sunset Boulevard and San Vicente. They booked Gilbert somewhere else, but then Gilly's time ran out, and he had no place to get to, so he stayed with me as we hung out in LA.

So Gilbert and I did Hollywood. We hadn't broken in yet; we were still just comics at The Improv, right? Now, we're just having fun in LA, goofing around doing stupid stuff. And Gilbert would walk everywhere. I said, "Gilly, it's LA. No one walks in Los Angeles." But I can remember driving down the street and seeing Gilbert walking around in LA like he was still in New York.

Working with Chris Albrecht, who was becoming my agent, I auditioned for parts on sitcoms and shows like *Mrs. Columbo*. I also took part in pilot projects—including one called *McGurk: A Dog's Life* created for NBC by Norman Lear. The concept was a show similar to *All in the Family* except we were all dogs. I'm thinking it's going to be "intellectually" that we're all dogs. But no, the idea was that we'd all be wearing dog costumes.

I remember one of the receptionists at the studio telling me, "Oh yeah, you look right for this part."

I'm going, "Nice, great, I look like a dog. Yeah."

I was mortified, but because NBC picked up the option to continue retaining me, I had to audition.

I called Albrecht: "You've got to get me out of this."

I got a classic Hollywood response: "Joe, you're there, it's going to be OK. No one's going to see it."

"I'm in a dog outfit," I said. "I can't break into the business in a dog outfit."

Anyhow, we shot the thing, and the audience stared at us like, "This is awful." Thank God it failed miserably. The pilot aired in June 1979—just that one episode, which, thankfully, I was not in—and the reviews were not kind.

Breaking Quick. Breaking Slow. Not Breaking at All.

When I think back to those first four and half years before I auditioned for *Saturday Night Live*, I realize just how lucky I was to break out when I did. Back in 1979, nobody knew who would make it out and make it big. Some broke early—like me.

Others broke later, and when they did, it was bigger than anyone could imagine. Larry David didn't break for another decade. I mean, you could see that genius mind all the way back then. Everybody thought of him as a brilliant Woody Allen type. But the *Seinfeld* pilot he cowrote with Jerry didn't air until 1989. Yet when his time came, he soared higher than the rest of us put together with *Seinfeld* and then *Curb Your Enthusiasm*. He and Jerry are now some of the wealthiest actors and comedians alive.

But the fascinating thing to have seen is that over 90 percent of the people who stood up on those stages and made people laugh—they never broke out at all. Who made it, who didn't make it . . . I saw guys I would love to bring onstage. And they were like your cleanup hitters. They were hysterical, hysterical guys. They must have been working on the road. I can remember their names, but they just never got big. I'm thinking, *How the hell did I make it? That guy is funnier than I ever could be, man.* You know? I mean, it's true that I worked hard and was really learning my craft. But when I remember guys with lots and lots of talent—guys you've never heard of but who had more talent than I did—I just have to feel grateful for the doors that opened and the breaks that came my way.

It was weird. Those guys were insanely funny cats, man. But they never surfaced, so you ask yourself, *How is that? How did that happen to them? And how did all this happen to me?*

To answer that question, I've got to take you to the famous 30 Rock studios of NBC where, for me, the engines really started to roar.

Part 3

LIVE FROM NEW YORK, IT'S SATURDAY NIGHT!

1980-1984

8

THE JERSEY GUY
AUDITIONS AT 30 ROCK

Summer 1980

I t was the summer of 1980, and a heat wave struck the US, killing several thousand people. President Jimmy Carter had the US boycott the Summer Olympics in Moscow because of their invasion of Afghanistan, and the Republican Party nominated Ronald Reagan (a fellow member of the Screen Actors Guild) as their nominee for president.

Me? I was happy continuing my emcee work at the comedy club, earning bank with the commercial gigs, and finishing up my second six-month stint being "on hold" with NBC. The network wanted to retain me for potentially using me and paid me to not go with anyone else. My son Joey was a year old, and Nancy was working as a legal secretary to support us—there's no way I would have made the leaps I did early on without Nancy. Life was good and just the right pace. As I sat poolside that summer, I never could have imagined that by year's end, I'd be doing impersonations of Carter on live, nationwide TV.

"I'm up at *Saturday Night Live* now," said John DeBellis, my good friend from The Improv. "I've been hired as a writer."

"Congratulations DeBellis! That's amazing," I said. "But how did that happen?"

Woody Allen had gotten his hands on DeBellis's writing and saw him at the clubs. Woody was close friends with a lady named Jean Doumanian who had worked at *SNL* under Lorne Michaels during its famous first five seasons.

There have been so many documentary videos and articles written about how it came to be that *SNL*'s creator, Lorne Michaels, left the show in May 1980. I don't want to revisit all that because I wasn't there and it's not my story to tell. But the essential facts are that Michaels got burnt out on producing the show, so at some point in the spring of 1980 he told NBC he was leaving. Head writer and future Senator Al Franken was probably Lorne's choice to pass the baton to, but that idea got axed when Franken scorched NBC's President and CEO Fred Silverman in a Weekend Update sketch called "A Limo for Lame-O." Apparently Silverman was furious and told NBC executive Brandon Tartikoff that Lorne was to blame. The season ended two weeks later: Lorne, the cast, and most of the staff departed from Studio 8H.

Did people want to leave? Did Lorne want to leave? I don't know. I don't know what the inside line was, but that's what they did.

Again, all this came before me and it's the stuff of TV journalists and historians to chronicle. In the moment, inquiring minds in the world of entertainment wanted to know: Would there be a sixth season of *SNL*? Where would new writers be found? Where would the show find comedians and actors to replace an entire cast? But the first question that needed an answer: Who would produce the show?

Enter Jean Doumanian, hired by Tartikoff after she was recommended for the job by another executive, Barbara Gallagher. With fewer than three months to go before the next season was to start,

Doumanian got right to work filling all the open slots, a task made difficult by NBC's cutting the *SNL* budget in half.

———

Let me backtrack here for a minute to explain something important. Christ Albrecht, who had managed The Improv and picked me to be a regular, had also become a talent agent at International Creative Management in 1980. Chris became my agent and was the agent for John DeBellis too. That was huge.

So, between Doumanian seeing DeBellis at the clubs and his connection to Woody Allen, *SNL* told Albrecht they wanted John as a writer for the show. They offered him $70,000, which was huge money for DeBellis at the time.

That's when Albrecht told me, "You got to get on *Saturday Night Live*." He told me they were paying $3,000 a week—but that was only for the weeks when there was a show.

I said, "Chris, I'm making more money doing commercials." I was doing so well doing commercials, I was making like eighty-five grand a year.

Besides, like I've said many times, I'm not a comic. And people in the business know it. George Carlin was a comic. Richard Pryor was a comic. Rodney Dangerfield was the best comic there ever was. Louie Anderson, Bob Saget—they were comics. Comics learn how to write and develop material. I was not a comic.

I was and am a working character actor, and I had learned to become an entertainer. I figured that I had my career going as a character actor and that maybe I'd do a film. All I wanted was just to work—not for the fame, having people recognize me. I never wanted to be a star. I just wanted to work.

Character actors are the third or fourth lead in an episodic show. They're not the lead or even the supporting actor—but they do support the show by their performance of eccentric, quirky, or offbeat roles. You're watching the show, and you see this character come across the stage or screen, and you think, *Hey, I know this guy.* You know him, but you can't remember his name.

That's all I wanted to be. So early on, I'd just go up onstage and display my craft in these characters, hoping an agent would be in the house and would think, *Hey, I could use this guy.*

One of my favorite actors was William Frawley who played Fred Mertz on *I Love Lucy.* Frawley was a utility guy, a supporting actor.

You're like the Robin to the Batman. People see you on a show and think, *Oh, I love that guy. What's his name?* You're not the star. You're kind of anonymous but still in the show business that you love. That was always my goal—not to become a star for crying out loud.

Chris Albrecht heard that I had misgivings about the chance I had to audition for *SNL.* "You've got to do this," he told me.

"Chris, you can't replace the original cast," I said. "You can't put me out there."

"Joe, don't be stupid. You're doing this damn show."

"All right boss," I said. "I trust you. I'll go in, but I don't feel good about this."

———

Doumanian and her new team were doing a whole sweep of the old comedy clubs but didn't pick anybody outright. Everyone wanted to get in the door at *SNL,* hoping to get a big break into the world of fame and fortune that the former cast members now inhabited. Hundreds—perhaps even a thousand—performers and comedians auditioned or were seen by Doumanian's team.

Jean knew she needed a utility guy like Danny Aykroyd for the cast, and that's when DeBellis told his new boss, "You should look at my friend Joe Piscopo for your utility guy."

A show like *SNL* needs to have some cast members who can jump into just about any skit to deliver a couple of lines or an impersonation that improves the sketch—but without upstaging the central character for the piece. Somebody has to play all these secondary characters, so DeBellis pitched me to *SNL*.

A few days after Doumanian saw me at The Improv, I was invited up to the seventeenth floor for a solo audition. Because of DeBellis, I passed about a thousand other people auditioning. And because I wasn't desperate for the income, I felt financially free enough to not be nervous about the whole thing. I did my Frank Sinatra impression for Jean, and she liked it well enough to invite me back for a full audition.

On August 28, I returned to 30 Rock, but this time I went up to the sixth floor—to the studio that was later to become David Letterman's home. There were about twenty of us as finalists, so at least half of us were going to get cut. I remember being so flippant and carefree and loose about the audition. I looked right into the camera and did two of the characters I had been developing at The Improv. First, I did a stereotype of a New York Yankees fan. Then I did a fellow named Paulie Herman—whom everyone now knows as Jersey Guy. (More on that in the next chapter.)

On September 1—without yet knowing whether I got the *SNL* job or not—I was booked on the Merv Griffin show for what would be my first network appearance. It wasn't Johnny Carson, but being on Merv's show was huge, a big break for me.

So out to California I went. I wasn't nervous, because even though Merv was a great guy, he wasn't one of my heroes. Also appearing on the show that night would be actor Steve Landesberg from the sitcom *Barney Miller*, Gregory Harrison of *Trapper John, M.D.* fame, and a pair of male strippers.

When it was my turn to perform, Merv goes, "Here's a guy from The Improv in New York City . . . Joe Piscopo."

One of my buddies who had been on Merv's show coached me, "Make sure you keep your eyes up, because you're going to want to look down at the audience, but the cameras are above the audience. And if you look down, you're not going to get eye contact." So I got up and fought the urge to look at the studio audience—instead looking straight into the audience watching at home. The shot was good. I did six minutes of material for my first network appearance. Boom! I did really well, by the grace of God. And in the back of my mind, I kept thinking how everybody back at the club would be watching.

Shortly after that, Albrecht called: "Congratulations, Joe! You've got the *SNL* job!"

———

Gilly also got hired—what are the odds? I mean, there were thousands of people who auditioned or got seen at the comedy clubs. And yet both of us got hired for *SNL*—just two goofball friends from the clubs.

And we were opposites. I was a family guy and Gilbert was a genius onstage, but he just couldn't really function in life. A total genius onstage, though. Where I was just an entertainer, he was a real true comic genius. And now we're on national television together. He was like my brother and we both made it.

A few days after getting hired, I went back to 30 Rock, this time up to the seventeenth floor where the *SNL* offices were located, to start meeting the other new hires.

And that's when I saw this young kid standing there—and I mean that literally because he wasn't even twenty.

"Hey, man. Joe Piscopo," I said.

"Hi, I'm Eddie Murphy."

We began talking and hit it off immediately because we made each other laugh. We had the same mindset, though from different backgrounds. Murphy was a nineteen-year-old from Long Island who had been doing stand-up since he was fifteen. And me, a not-yet-thirty guy from Jersey, with four years of comedy clubs, character sketches, and commercials under my belt.

The producers pulled me aside and said, "Hey Joe, will you do us a favor? We don't know whether or not we're going to hire Eddie. Will you do a sketch with him?"

"Absolutely," I said. "What skit do you have in mind?"

"The Richard Pryor and Chevy Chase 'Word Association' sketch. We want to see what Eddie can do."

The humor in the sketch goes right into the issue of race—and does so in such a way that networks today would never allow. Pryor acts the part of a job applicant, giving an interview to Chevy Chase's character. The interview ends with a "psychological test" where Chase says a word and Pryor is to say the first word that comes to mind in response. Chevy throws one racist term after another to Richard, who gets more and more agitated. It was a hilarious sketch.

The producers gave the script to me and Eddie and told us to do a read-through of the sketch.

Eddie played Pryor's part, obviously, and he just freaking smoked it. Just killed it.

I remember telling some of them, "This is the new Richard Pryor. You can see that at first glance."

Even so, the producers were unsure of what to do with Eddie: "He's a little edgy" was their line. He was politically incorrect and said what he wanted to say. Did I mention he was nineteen? Also, let's not shy away from the idea that the network was afraid to have a person of color being that edgy and in your face—this was 1980.

I loved it and I advocated for him from the first day. *SNL* was known for being edgy and political, so it seemed odd to keep Murphy on the sidelines. But that's what happened at first. They hired Eddie as a "featured player" to start, not a "cast member" who was guaranteed to be on every show and in multiple skits.

———

It's amazing how fast things move in show business. On October 23, 1980, Brandon Tartikoff and Jean Doumanian gathered us six new cast members together for a press conference breakfast. A staff writer from my hometown newspaper, *The Herald News*, summed it up well:

> Piscopo, whose father Joseph practices law in Passaic, joins Denny Dillon, Gilbert Gottfried, Gail Matthius, Ann Risely and Charles Rocket in the stock company, and if your first tendency is to ask "Who?" remember that five years ago Gilda Radner, John Belushi, Dan Aykroyd, Bill Murray, Garrett Morris, Chevy Chase, Jane Curtin, and Laraine Newman were also totally unknown.[13]

To press home the point further, the writer added this philosophical musing about the ebb and flow of fame: "It might even be reasonable to assume that in five more years a few members of both the old and new casts will again be firmly ensconced in the ranks of the unknown!"

In other words, nobody knew who we were, but everybody knew we were tasked with one of the most impossible assignments in television history: To replace the original cast of *Saturday Night Live*.

9

I'VE GOT THE WORLD ON A STRING

SNL Season 6 | 1980-1981

Was I scared? No, I was terrified.

I kept thinking, *My goal is simply to survive this.* From that insecurity, everything was done out of fear.

Please don't take this the wrong way, because I know that show business isn't equivalent to military service or the awfulness of active combat. But I've talked on my radio show to Colonel Jack Jacobs, a good friend and a Medal of Honor recipient, about his experiences in the Vietnam War. He told me about being in the middle of battle and having to drag his buddies out of the rice fields when air support couldn't get to them in time to survive. I asked him, "What were you thinking? What was going through your mind?"

He said, "Joey, you'd be amazed what fear can do for you. Fear is a big motivation."

Well, on a much lesser, minuscule note, that's how I felt during the lead-up days as I headed into the beginning of my first season of *SNL*, that ill-fated sixth season of the show. It was just fear.

And from that emotion, you work hard to get your words down, to practice your performance, and to do it the best that you can. I pushed too hard that whole season, and I don't recall having much fun at all. There was fear and also an immense respect—you just didn't want to mess up the legacy of *Saturday Night Live*. This thought was searing itself in my brain: *Let me not mess this up.*

What I mostly remember is the feeling that I didn't belong there. I kept thinking, *Let me just do this as best as I can because it's going to end quickly, and then I'll move on with my life.*

First Show

Speaking of job loss, we opened the season on November 15, 1980, just eleven days after Ronald Reagan's landslide defeat of Jimmy Carter. And right there, in one of the first sketches of the new *SNL* era, I impersonated Jimmy Carter standing in the Oval Office contemplating his election loss. The humor of the sketch is that Rosalyn Carter (played by Ann Risley) is happy he lost because she can get her husband back (and into bed) from the stressful job. My Jimmy, however, was oblivious to his wife's seductions.

Later in that show, I impersonated Congressman John Anderson, who ran for president that year and earned almost 7 percent of the vote as an independent. When the *SNL* writers told me about the skit and assigned me to do Anderson, I asked, "Who in the name of goodness gracious is John Anderson?"

Back then, prepping for an impersonation of someone you knew nothing about meant hitting the rewind button over and over as you worked your way through a pile of VHS tapes. There was no YouTube. You just had to slog it out, watching the film to find the person's subtle trademark quirks and nuances—like a caricature artist does. If I did my job well, the audience would get it—and laugh. And more often than not, they did.

Sports Guy & Eddie's Launch

SNL's comedy—especially in those beginning years—is rooted in parodies of pop culture and making fun of what people watched on TV every night.

This was before 24/7 sports news went mainstream on cable TV and the internet (ESPN launched in 1979). Being a sports junky, I wanted to mock how the sports news guy on local TV would get about three minutes to catch viewers up on everything that happened in sports that day. Working with our go-to *SNL* writer Barry Blaustein, I became the loud-volume, staccato-talking sports news broadcaster who broke in for a segment on the Weekend Update sketches that season.

> *Hello again, everybody.*
> *Joe Piscopo.*
> *Live.*
> *Saturday Night Sports.*
> *The big story? . . .*

The sportscaster routine got a lot of laughs and gave me the chance to partner with Eddie Murphy for what became his first speaking bit on national TV. After the first two shows, Eddie still hadn't had a speaking line (he was in the background of a sketch in Week 2), even though everyone in the *SNL* offices had awakened to the brilliance of this local nineteen-year-old from Long Island. So, in prep for the season's third show (December 6), Eddie says, "I want to do a sketch."

I go, "What are you thinking?"

In real life, a Cleveland judge that week ruled that all high school basketball teams had to have two white players. Eddie said he wanted to tackle that—and hit it squarely on racial lines. For his first time speaking on live, national TV.

So we developed a Sports Guy sketch where I would mention the court ruling and then introduce Eddie as "Raheem Abdul

Muhammad"—a high school basketball player from Cleveland—
for commentary.

Sports Guy: *What's the story, Raheem?*

Eddie sits to my left, perched on top of some telephone books to
make him seem like a tall basketball player. He looks right into the
camera and speaks with a ghetto-stereotype accent and grammar.

Raheem: *Yo, baby. Look, I've been a junior at Cleveland High*
going on seven years now. I'd like to tell y'all that this is the most
disgusting thing y'all done pulled up to date.

We ain't got much. I say least let us have basketball. Is noth-
ing sacred? Anytime we get something going good, y'all got to
move in on it.

In the sixties, we wore platform shoes. Then y'all had to wear
platform shoes. In the early seventies, we braided our hair. Then
in the late seventies, y'all had to braid your hair. Now it's 1980.
We on welfare and by the end of next year, y'all going to be on
welfare too.

After Eddie says that line about welfare, the audience roars with
laughter, louder and longer than they had at any point in the season.
Eddie pauses for a full ten seconds, then concludes:

Raheem: *I don't see no judge saying that every two bathroom*
attendants got to be white. All I'm saying is that y'all stay on the
hockey courts and the polo fields and let us stay on the basketball
courts because, if God wouldn't have wanted whites to be equal
to blacks, everybody have one of these.

With this, Eddie pulls out one of those big 1980s "boom box" radios.
The crowd goes nuts.

You could feel the electricity of the moment. Eddie and I turn our
heads and look at each other—and somehow, we keep in character.

I wink at him, acknowledging to my new friend what he had just pulled off—for himself . . . and for the entire show, really.

From that moment, it was like maybe all of us in the cast began to believe we had a shot at not screwing up the season. Follow Eddie, and let's build this together. When you're next to stardom, you know it.

The synergy and the love were there—at least at first (more on that later).

There's one more thing I'll never forget about that moment. Right before we go onstage and slide into those news desk chairs, as we're standing close together backstage, I hear Eddie whisper to himself.

That's when it hit me. Here Eddie was, all of nineteen years old and getting ready to stand in front of eight to ten million viewers. (Riding the wave of popularity from the first five seasons, we hit Nielsen ratings of 9.8 that season—the fourth highest in the show's history.) But Eddie's mind isn't on millions of invisible viewers. He takes joy in thinking about what his old classmates from high school would think when they saw him.

Eddie whispers it again: "The kids at Roosevelt High are never going to believe this."

Jersey Guy

On that same night, I debuted my Paulie Herman / Jersey Guy character I had developed during my stand-up career.

I based Jersey Guy on an actual person I met by chance years earlier on a road trip with my wife. We were about to get onto a ferry to cross a river somewhere in the South. I must have said something about New Jersey because all of a sudden, I heard this high-pitched, squeaky, rapid, Jersey accent saying to me, "Hey! Hey! You're from Jersey? I'm from Jersey."

"Yes, yes. I'm from Jersey," I said to the woman.

And that's when the classic Jersey question came out of her mouth—a question that makes sense to everyone from Jersey: "What exit? What exit?"

Because that's how we identify each other, you know? What exit off the highway are you from?

The sketch went over so well that night that we used Jersey Guy five more times that season and once the next.

Overexposure? It's a real thing when you're doing these bits— the reality that maybe people are getting tired of a character. I started hearing that some people didn't like the character. That Jersey Guy would have worked in a prime-time sitcom, but it wasn't *SNL* material.

It's interesting how word got around back then, even before smartphones and social media. The comedy community is a small community—everybody knows everything about what's going on in the business, so I heard from the grapevine that Jimmy Belushi (who later joined *SNL* but at the time was up in Chicago with Second City), didn't like Jersey Guy sketches because they were too over the top. Second City was, and is, a revered comedy troop, and you have to respect the voices from the guild enough to respond to feedback.

Fans loved the bit, but I guess it was just too silly—whatever. Some people criticizing Paulie were the kings of comedy at the time, so we listened to what they said and killed the guy off the next season. But not before Jersey Guy got us into trouble with a real-life Jersey mayor.

In the second to last show of the season, we did a prerecorded short film where Paulie went around showing off the highlights of his beloved New Jersey. I put my brother, Richie, in it, having him be a worker at a chemical plant in Piscataway. In a Homer Simpson way, we had a white substance fall off his helmet and onto his sandwich at lunch—but he still ate it. If all you knew about Piscataway was this sketch, you'd think it was full of chemical factories and idiots.

The town's mayor went ballistic. He mailed letters to the governor and the FCC, complaining about NBC and threatening further action.

The network promptly sent a letter of apology, but it all hit the news and was great publicity. We planned to use the material during the next Weekend Update and invite the mayor to be on the show.

But then the wheels started falling off the season.

The Infamous F-Bomb Show

The February 21, 1981, show *could* have been epic for all the right reasons.

First, Eddie debuted his now-legendary "Mr. Robinson's Neighborhood" ghetto parody of the *Mister Rogers' Neighborhood* PBS show. That character returned nine more times in the four seasons Eddie was on *SNL*, and then again thirty-five years later when he hosted *SNL* in 2019.

Eddie was also very excited about the musical guest that night. In rehearsals, he says to me, "Prince is on the show this week!" with big eyes.

And I go, "Great! Who is he?"

He goes, "No, you don't understand. It's Prince, man."

This was all before Prince took off and became one of the bestselling artists ever. Give credit to our producer, Jean, for getting these great musical guests and hosts on the show that year.

But all anyone remembers about that show was how Charles Rocket dropped an f-bomb during the closing credits. As the show ended, Charles was in a wheelchair, still in character from the sketch that had just ended where he played JR from the TV show *Dallas*. This was when the "Who shot JR?" cliffhanger happened—one of those really big TV events of the decade that everyone remembers.

So, as the closing credits begin, Charles says, "Aw, man, it's the first time I've ever been shot in my life. I'd like to know who the F--- did it."

I know that seems like a small thing now, but this is 1981. That word never got into prerecorded shows—and even though live TV can utilize a "five-second delay" mechanism, allowing censors to bleep out anything inappropriate—*SNL* has only rarely used a time delay. And they weren't using one that night.

I remember standing onstage there next to Charlene Tilton, the host that night, and thinking I didn't hear it clearly. I thought, *There's no way he really said that.* It happened so quickly live, I said to someone, "Did he really say it? He couldn't have really said it." And then it was like, "Oh my God, he did it—he said the *F*-word on TV."

Of course, Paul Shaffer did the same thing once in a previous season as part of the *SNL* band. And some people think Prince muttered the word in his song that night. So it wasn't really the first time. But oh my gosh, that was all the impetus NBC needed. They weren't happy with the show already, and I think they used that F-bomb as an excuse to plan how they'd start whacking everyone.

The gang was all still together for the next show on March 7. We cold-opened with one of those self-referential (metanarrative) sketches where we're talking about the show itself. The whole cast sat in what was supposed to be a backstage room with that night's host, Bill Murray—one of the stars from the original cast.

He's telling us to not get bothered about all the negative reviews of the show and how badly the season had gone so far, and how much better the original cast was. He went around the room to each cast member, giving them advice from a veteran.

He turned to me last: "Are you going to stick with Joe Piscopo as your name?"

Yeah, I stuck with the name.

Twenty years later, when TV critic Tom Shales interviewed me, I had this to say about my first season of *SNL*:

> I could never describe to you in words how painful those first ten months really were. You just knew that this was America's favorite television show, and yet here we were, taking it right into the toilet.
>
> Saturday night, after the show, it was pretty much like a funeral, like you were mourning. Oh my God, oh my God, did we really do this, oh my God—and then we had to turn it around on Monday all over again.[14]

We had nothing, and we had everything. We had the world on a string.

But was NBC going to stick with us? The handwriting seemed to be on the wall.

Enter Dick Ebersol

Jean's twelve-episode run as executive producer—and six years altogether with *SNL*, having worked on the show since its inception—ended when BT and Silverman hired Dick Ebersol. Dick had helped Lorne launch the original show, so there seemed to be some logic to his taking over—though he's no Lorne.

We had failed miserably. We were all vilified by the younger generation for ruining their favorite television show.

Immediately, Charles, Ann, and Gilbert got fired. Gilly never would look up at the camera. He would always go into his riffs, looking down at the floor, which really doesn't work on television. So they fired Gilbert. They didn't see his genius because I guess they needed the success immediately during that first year. At any rate, Gilbert went on to be a legend and have constant work anyway. When he passed away, while I was writing this book, it really rocked me because I didn't even know he was sick. RIP Gilly.

Ebersol also moved out almost all the writers, including my buddy DeBellis. Gone. One more episode later, Denny and Gail got axed.

Very talented people: fired, fired, fired.

Eddie and I were sitting there, taking it all in, and waiting for our turn in the firing line.

"You want to get out of here?" Eddie asked me. We were going to go do a hit at a local comedy club.

"Yeah, let's go."

Then Dick comes out and points his finger at us: "Eddie. Joe. In my office. Now."

After all that we had been through that season—all the crap thrown at us and the bad reviews and lack of support, even from NBC—the only thing left was to get canned and move on. Why be upset now? Like I said earlier, at the beginning of the season, I had not expected this whole *SNL* thing to last.

So Eddie and I walked into Dick's office all nonchalant and said, "You know, boss, we were about to—"

"Gentlemen, this is how it is. We've decided to keep both of you."

After firing all these incredible people, Ebersol was giving us the break of our lives—and we couldn't care less.

The two of us had such a flippant attitude and carried that confident cockiness right into the next season—and it worked. The me of today would have gone in and kissed the ring. But back then I didn't know any better.

Eddie and I go, "OK. Whatever. Fine. Now, we've got to go Dick—we've got to get to a club. Anything else you need?"

10

IT'S NOT A TUMOR

December 1981–January 1982

S ometimes you just can't catch a break in life.

With that rough first year at *SNL* behind us, we began to see signs of success during the fall shows of the 1981–1982 season. I felt looser on the set and was beginning to enjoy the fruits of the showbiz success. Joey was two, and I enjoyed being a dad.

But shortly after Thanksgiving, I struggled with a sore throat, so I went to my brother-in-law, Dr. Olaf Haroldson, who was an ear, nose, and throat doc. He takes a look and says, "You know, you got a little tumor or something in there."

"Wait, what?" I say.

"You've got something growing on your thyroid. You should get it checked out."

I go to Columbia Presbyterian, where a doctor takes a long needle, drives it in my throat, and takes a biopsy. They get back the results and inform me, "We think it's cancer. You need to have surgery."

I made the appointment and didn't tell anybody outside of family except Eddie—and maybe Dick Ebersol. I don't think I even told them the details. I just said, "I've got to go get operated on." I didn't tell the rest of the cast anything.

Back then, you didn't talk about these things with colleagues—at least I didn't. In fact, I never talked about my cancer in interviews for a decade even after my diagnosis. I didn't want people to think I was dying.

So we did the show on December 12 with Billy Murray hosting. I did a Sports Guy segment where I interviewed Eddie as a 1981 Muhammad Ali—then threw back to a black-and-white "vintage newsreel" of us as younger versions. Eddie had resisted using prosthetics before that night (which is interesting given his later success with the prosthetics-heavy movie *The Klumps*). Eddie as Ali is one of his best-loved impersonations of all time.

All of this is so vivid to me even now because it's surreal to be performing live entertainment in front of millions of people while also thinking about a pending surgery and the potential for a life-altering or life-ending cancer diagnosis.

I did the show that night and got up the next morning to do a hit on NBC's *NFL Today* with Bryant Gumble, who had a cameo on *SNL* the week before.

Then I went to the hospital for surgery. My wife, brother, father, and mother were all there to see me go into surgery. A priest came in before surgery to pray. I hadn't been an active, practicing Catholic since high school and I felt like a hypocrite.

"Father, am I supposed to pray now because I might have cancer?"

He just looked at me like, "Oh, here's another jerk with all the answers."

As the bed carried me down the hallway into surgery, I did a Boris Karloff Frankenstein impression, sitting up in the gurney to make everyone laugh.

They took out the tumor and half the thyroid. They had to take the nerve of the vocal cord, place it on my shoulder, and then operate on the thyroid because the vocal cord is wrapped around the thyroid. One wrong snip of the scalpel would mean I'd lose my career: no singing, acting, voice-overs for commercials—all would be gone.

But all went well, and when I woke up my wife, Nancy, was there and broke the news to me: "Joe, it's not malignant. It's OK. It's benign."

So I was real cocky, thinking, *Great. It's benign. It's nothing. Of course it's benign—I'm only thirty-one years old.*

All this was happening while *SNL* was on a monthlong break for Christmas. I told my wife we should take Joey and get away for a couple of weeks to Montauk on Long Island.

But then, Dr. Rock Positano, a medical intern at the time and one of my dearest friends to this day, told me to get a second opinion. Being the hypochondriac that I am, I didn't need persuading. So they FedExed the tumor down to Positano and Dr. Manny Blum at NYU, and they studied the little ball of benigness.

Except that it wasn't.

I get a call from the doctor saying, "Oh, we were wrong. It's not benign. It's cancer."

They cut into it, and they found a medullary carcinoma, which is a very aggressive form of cancer.

Can you believe that?

———

Now, compared to heroes who battle horrific cancers that ravage their bodies, this was nothing like that. But at the same time, whenever you hear that "Big *C*" word, it changes your whole life. It was the most frightening thing I had ever gone through in my short life. And going through that experience changed my life.

Before this, I had always worked to stay healthy. I never took drugs. Never used cocaine—which is saying a lot, being an early cast member of *SNL*. I drank only in moderation.

But once that cancer scare happened, I read and practiced all I could to keep it at bay. I'm not giving medical guidance here, but they recommended I eat a lot of leafy green vegetables and take high doses of certain vitamins. And back then, they also were saying to work out with weights because they thought that fat tended to breed tumors.

I said, "You mean, if I work out, maybe I can stave this thing off a little bit?"

And that's the origin of my getting into weightlifting. (More on that later.)

Of course, they also told me to take radiation to burn out any possible remaining cancer.

"Can you guarantee this radiation won't kill me?" I asked.

I didn't like the answers I got, so I opted out of the radiation plan. But that came with its own risk—the possible return of the cancer.

They had another reason for thinking I was crazy for skipping the radiation. If cancer resurfaced and they had to cut on me again, I stood in danger of having damage to the nerves that control the vocal cords. With me earning a living doing all the characters and all the singing I did with impersonations—more radiation or a second surgery could jeopardize all that.

It's weird because I had just turned thirty and felt so alive on the one hand, right? You feel like you've got your whole life ahead of you. I was in the middle of my second *SNL* season and continued to do the lucrative commercials. On the other hand, the docs said, "Don't forget Joe, you could still die from this. Cancers come back all the time."

But it was too scary for me, so I stayed away from the radiation and submitted to frequent testing—which I still do to this day. After the first decade of being cancer-free, they told me that since there hadn't been any return, I was in the clear.

To this day, I keep my fingers crossed and am still very careful with my health—and by the grace of God, I'm still alive and well.

────────

The cancer scare also changed me on the inside. It permanently altered my idea of success. Your priorities change. You lose track of your original goals in life.

Because the death threat of cancer's return hung over me, I began to take a short-term perspective on my career. I'll talk about this more later, but I began to opt out of learning and working the Hollywood system. Doors started to close, and I didn't care.

Looking back now I feel this cancer was a direct message between the eyes for me from God. And I missed it. I skirted a bullet, but what did I do in response? I got mad that I had gone through this situation and wasn't even in the clear. God was sending me a message to stay on the straight and narrow path and to concentrate on what I was doing with my family and career. I can see that message now—with age comes wisdom—but at the time I just missed it.

I wanted to enjoy life and have fun because I felt such a sense of mortality.

I thought I was going to die by thiry-five. I was convinced of it. So that's where my life changed, right then.

Had I not been diagnosed with cancer, I probably would've been more concentrated on my career. I would have thought more long term—on how to maintain the showbiz life. But I thought I was dying, and unfortunately, I did dumb things as a result. You think, *I'm not going to live, and who cares anyway because I'm dying.*

And then as I survived and a decade passed, I began to think, *Oh wait. I may be here a while longer after all.* And then I tried to play catch-up and rebuild all the bridges that I may have burned in Hollywood. But we'll get to that later.

Eddie, Robin, and I cutting up during promos for SNL.

David Lee Roth. David Brenner. Carl Wilson. Is that an Ed Norton shirt I'm wearing?

"A Really Big Shew." With the awesome Stevie Wonder and me as Ed Sullivan. SNL.

Me and Dick Cavett in LA. Love that guy.

Me and "The Donald" back in the day.

Love my fugazy 80s glitter tux tie. At the MTV Awards.

*Kimberly, the mother of
Allie, Mikey, and Olivia.*

*My true hero, Pasquale
Giuseppe Piscopo. My Pop.*

How cool was my Pop?

Eddie as olympian Carl Lewis in my first HBO Special "I'm Carl Lewis!"

I know what you're thinking, but honestly, I just wanted to meet the true GOAT, Michael Jordan.

With dear friend Danny Aiello and Leonardo DiCaprio.

Dear pal and Yankee super legend Yogi Berra was one of the funniest guys on the planet!

Such respect and appreciation for this brilliant gal, Maria Bartiromo.

Two baseball heroes, Johnny Bench and Don Mattingly.

With a mentor and friend—the great Steve Forbes.

Frank Sinatra's youngest daughter, a brilliant producer, and a talent in her own right, Tina Sinatra.

Brent Spiner is really great and one funny guy. At a Star Trek Convention in Vegas.

That's me and awesome comedian, Jeff Norris touring devastating damage from superstorm Sandy.

At Wildwood, NJ. Appreciated President Trump granting this Jersey guy the first welcoming interview in my home state!

NFL Hall of Famers, Franco Harris and Joe Theisman. NJ Hall of Fame.

Stacy. Takin' care of business.

With dear friend and superstar attorney Mr. Anthony Pope.

Mentor and lifelong pal Raymond Mirra.

With American Hero Jerry Padgett, FDNY Legend Sal Cassano, and Mikey! Tunnel to Towers.

Always love working with Andy and the Atomic Pearl Orchestra. Man, they can swing!

With Charley's mom heading into
The Plaza for the SNL 40th. NYC.

"It's a quarter to three. . . ."

Hoboken, NJ—The magnificent Carolyn
Palmer designed statue of Frank Sinatra.

My guiding light. May she always
Rest In the Lord's Peace. Momma
Mia, Edith Ida Piscopo.

A la Mr. Sinatra. NJ State Police style!

Honored and humbled to be presented with this very special Flag of the United States by US Army Staff Sargaent Stine for proudly supporting our Troops.

Supporting our POW-MIA Heroes.

Joey Benefit! Those are my Dad's cufflinks!

The Columbus Day Parade in New York City!

Proud to be the Grand Marshall for the Philadelphia Italian American Parade!   *Sicily*

La Famiglia e molte importante! Family is everything.

Daddy daughter dance!

My big boy, Joey!

My favorite thing to do—hangin' with all my children at home.

Best. Dog. Ever. Otis.

Dear Mom and family with Cardinal Dolan outside of St. Patrick's in NYC.

Grandma and the kids.

Allie, Charley, Mikey, and Olivia. And one proud Pop.

La Famiglia di Piscopo.

11

EDDIE

One of the glorious joys I've had in my life is working with Eddie Murphy on live TV. The spontaneity you saw was all natural. Anything could happen because we had no tape delay.

When you're next to somebody in the groove, you know it, and it is exciting. I can't even describe it fully to you—though I'm going to try!

Eddie is one of the smartest, most intuitive, brightest stars I've ever known. He finds a lot of material organically because he has the ability to understand the common man and woman. There are only a couple of people like that I've ever worked with.

To me, he's always going to be the funniest guy on any stage he's on. I know I'm biased because I came up with him, but when I saw him explode like that it was amazing. We came into *SNL* together but were so different. I was twenty-eight and he was nineteen. Can you believe that? I looked at this guy, and I remember thinking, *God, bless this little kid, man. He's going to go forever.* And it was such a joy to work with him those four seasons of *SNL*.

Eddie was a comic genius. Look, I consider myself a working entertainer and feel confident I can hold my own. I'll sweat it out, give you my all, and I'm pretty sure you're going to walk away having been entertained.

But guys like Eddie are in another universe. Amazing talent. He would do his bits. He would do his voices. He would go right up into the camera with his energy, and then he would wait—and that was your cue. Eddie owned natural instincts for the rhythm of comedy and for knowing what audiences would think was funny.

I remember in the fall of 1981, during the early weeks of our second season on *SNL*, Eddie and I were working in our *SNL* office, tossing out ideas and just cutting up and having a good time.

Eddie turned to me and said, "Hey man, I'm going to do Buckwheat." He started in explaining the idea for what we all know as his famous impersonation of Buckwheat from *The Little Rascals*.

As long as I could remember, the original Rascals shows had been criticized for the Buckwheat character because of his heavy dialect and the way he mispronounced words. These all reinforced stereotypes.

I said, "Eddie, all due respect, but it might be a little racist, don't you think?"

Eddie said, "Nah, man. I'm doing it. I'm doing it—and it's going to be something everyone's talking about."

I loved that about Eddie. He not only had the creative spark but also the courage to launch big new concepts and characters.

What's ironic is how similar our *SNL* cast was to the kids who made up the Rascals: four to six white kids and one black kid.

Today, would the networks even allow a barely twenty-year-old comedian to do a skit like Eddie's Buckwheat—with all its racial messaging? I don't know, but he debuted the character on October 10, 1981, exactly one year after the death of Billy Thomas, the actor who played Buckwheat—isn't that a weird coincidence? Buckwheat launched in the fall of that important second season of our *SNL* experience when we needed big, quick wins. And the character turned out to be a huge thing for Eddie and for us. From then on, wherever Eddie went, people asked him to do Buckwheat.

Ebony and Ivory

It's interesting that we became such good friends because we are total opposites. Eddie is intrinsically cool. I am a dork dad. I would go right home after the show and take care of my kid. But I think that's why we hung out and got along.

I remember one Christmas morning, hearing a knock at the door and Eddie coming over with gifts for me and Joey and Nancy. I was like the dopey suburban guy, and Eddie was the smooth cat, man.

He would go, "Hey, come over to my house."

This was just at the start of his breaking out, and he still lived with his family. He'd drive me out to Long Island in his 280ZX. We'd be together all the time.

"I'm with Eddie," I would tell Nancy.

We went to the local recreational center where Eddie would hang out. He wanted to show me where he grew up. And while he's standing there, nobody came over to him. They're looking at him like, "Who the heck are you?"

And I'm like, "That's rude. So, what's up with that, Eddie?"

He goes, "I got out." Then he turned and walked away.

I felt for Eddie and understood completely because it reminded me that the same thing happened to Frank Sinatra when he went to Hoboken. They gave him the same attitude.

So then, one day, this happened: We were watching movies together at an apartment he had just moved into. First time living out on his own. He's breaking out—now twenty.

Then he looks up; he's looking outside this high rise, and he goes, "Oh crap."

I go, "What happened?"

Someone from the neighborhood had thrown paint on his car. He bought that new Datsun 280ZX and they threw paint on it.

So that's the love his home neighborhood showed him at first—just jealous of him. That's what I saw. And he never talked about it.

"Eddie, I'm taking you to Jersey with me," I said. "This is bullshit. They should kiss your feet around here for what you've done. You're getting out."

We Piscopos lived in a little town called Alpine. I bought my first house there. Now it's where all the stars are. But I went there when it was just regular people. It was a very northeast-tip-of-Jersey little town.

Eddie found the best house in town. It was a pretty big house back then. And he was two minutes away.

He drove an Excalibur, one of these big cars, and he'd come rolling down the street to our house to hang out. We would do stupid videos and play piano.

And I would go to his house. We would wash his cars. Play music. Anything. It would be two o'clock in the morning, and he didn't want me to leave. "No, you got to hang out."

It was a great time. And he was a great friend.

———

I remember one Wednesday when we were having "read through" day at *SNL* the day when we'd sit in a room together and get familiar with the scripts for the upcoming show.

We had all started making some money, and I had my mind on a Jaguar XJS—a 12-cylinder monster that I wanted to buy.

In the middle of me talking about the car, Eddie goes, "What's that Joe?"

I had the brochure. I said, "Look at this car."

He goes, "Oh, man, that's beautiful. I'm getting one too. Let's go."

So we left, and we went and bought matching Jaguars.

He got a white one. I got a black one.

Ebony and ivory in the Jaguars.

Then we raced back to New York to get back to rehearsal.

————

Stevie Wonder hosted the show at the end of the 1983 season—one of the few times the host was also the musical guest. Stevie and Eddie were both big at that point, and they had gotten very close in their friendship.

Later, after we finished one of the shows in the fall of 1983, Eddie comes over to me and he goes, "Joe, you're a dork. You got to chill out. I'm taking you to see Stevie at Radio City Music Hall tomorrow night."

So Sunday night comes. We're in the audience, and Stevie Wonder is up onstage entertaining six thousand people.

Stevie goes into a riff: "Going on a campaign for love." And the crowd is repeating him. Back and forth. This went on to be one of my first comedy bits.

Going on a campaign. I'm going on a campaign for love.

Stevie stops playing. He says, "Eddie Murphy and Joe Piscopo are here tonight. Guys come up onstage."

Eddie drags my butt onstage. He's wearing skintight leather pants. I'm wearing Dockers.

Stevie starts singing again, in this R&B soul style, "Going on a campaign. Going on a campaign," and then says, "Eddie, you try."

Eddie—cool as ever—leans into the mic and sings, "Going on a campaign for love"—in his own voice, but in the same style as Stevie.

Then Stevie says, "Joe, you try it."

I take the mic. I can do this. I know how to sing for people. I do it all the time.

But when I sing the lines, they come out crooning like Sinatra: "I'm go-ing on a campaign . . . for loooove."

The band stops playing.

I'm looking over at Eddie.

Eddie's staring at me, like only he can do.

Even Stevie's staring at me.

I was a dork dad onstage with two cool cats.

B-U-U-H-F

Eddie and I would do this thing where if a sketch didn't work, we would just very quietly let out a low breath through our lips. It would come out like you could spell it: B-U-U-H-F. It was about like that.

So if something wasn't working, he would make that sound, and it would be all I could do to not pee in my pants.

Like, "Whoa, that didn't work," we would say without words— just a look in our eyes and the sound, B-U-U-H-F.

That was a running joke with us.

Fast-forward thirty-five years. In 2019, Eddie returned to *SNL* for the first time since our departure at the end of the 1983–1984 season. I was backstage during the rehearsal, and I heard that Eddie had arrived.

"What's that? Eddie's here? Let me go see Eddie."

So I went and found him, and we hugged.

"Hey, man," I said.

He leans in and says into my ear, "B-U-U-H-F."

Ha! That was our thing still, after all those years. He never forgot that, baby.

12

CRAZY. MAN. CRAZY.

SNL Season 7 | 1981-1982

S o my second season on *SNL* featured a new boss, Dick Ebersol, and an entirely new cast (except for Eddie). Technically, Robin Duke, Tim Kazurinsky, and Tony Rosato had begun the previous season, joining in with us after Jean's firing. But we produced only one show before the writer's strike ended that season (literally, the strike began while we were on the air). Dick then added Christine Ebersole and Mary Gross to the cast, and he brought in a whole new team of writers.

Dick landed us premier musical acts that year, giving us some much-needed star power mojo: Rod Stewart, Billy Joel, Olivia Newton-John, Elton John, John Cougar Mellencamp, Luther Vandross, Hall & Oates, and Johnny Cash. With the launch of MTV on cable in 1981, singers and bands knew their fans wanted to *see* performances when they turned on the television. *SNL* had become a pathway for musicians to connect to the much-coveted demographic of young audiences.

By the end of my second season, the *SNL* ship had turned itself around from the previous year's fiascos. I know that not everyone is a fan of the Ebersol years of *SNL* (1981–1985), distinct as they are from the Lorne Michaels flavor of production. He and I didn't always agree, but you've got to give Dick credit for running the show with professionalism and creativity. In entertainment, you can't just slavishly copy what came before, and under Ebersol's leadership, we experimented with new ideas.

And boy did we ever have a lot of new ideas that we launched that season. Many of these starred Eddie by himself or paired with me: Gumby (and later me as Pokey), Solomon & Solomon, Velvet Jones, and Buckwheat.

Eddie was fearless and went straight into the heart of race issues in America, like with his character Tyrone Green he debuted that fall in the now legendary "Prose and Cons" sketch. Eddie played Green, an imprisoned criminal who had become a published and acclaimed poet. Green looks right into the camera and recites his poem from his maximum-security cell about how he would kill his landlord, concluding with:

> *Kill my landlord.*
> *Kill my landlord.*
> *C-I-L-L my landlord.*

You could sense the increasing star power of Eddie by the screams and applause whenever his name was called out in the opening montage. And Hollywood was already calling for him too. Such energy.

Diverticulitis

That season, I added a half dozen new impressions of celebrities and newsmakers. I became the go-to impersonator of President Ronald Reagan. And in the season opener, I debuted "A Few Minutes with Andy Rooney," where I impersonated Rooney doing his famous *60*

Minutes opinion pieces. I heard later that Rooney hated these bits, but I'm sure I could have gotten him on my side if I had gotten a few minutes with him.

But that season's biggest winner for me was "The Whiners"—a married couple who everyone in the sketch (and the audience) came to love to hate. Doug and Wendy Whiner (played by Robin Duke) spoke everything they said with a whining voice and full of nasal obnoxiousness. They complained about everything that happened to them in a sketch—even things that should have been positive, they'd find a way to whine about.

How did we come up with the Whiners? Simple. We were working all through the night, struggling to produce material. Writing sketches. Scrapping sketches. Feeling miserable.

Robin and I were in her office in the writer's wing, and we started complaining about the work. One of us started using a loud nasal voice just for kicks, and the other mirrored.

"Oh, it's so late," I said. "What are we going to write?"

"I can't think of anything."

"I don't have anything either."

"Oh no. We're going to get fired."

"That would be awful."

"You know what's awful? These sketches we've written."

"Dick is going to can us."

"We'll lose our jobs."

"We'll lose our house."

We kept it going and that's how "The Whiners" came into being—just the two of us whining about our jobs. It was as simple as that.

Robin had the idea for the Whiners to have some sort of affliction. What's a good affliction? What's funny? I said, "Diverticulitis is funny—I mean, the word itself is funny." So that became our catchphrase, pronounced as obnoxiously as possible: "We've got di-ver-tic-u-li-tis."

The Whiners would appear on *SNL* ten times over the next three seasons. And with all due respect to Dick, I've always thought that if the Whiners had come around when Lorne was producing the show, we might have done a couple of "Whiner" movies, the way Lorne's production company has turned so many *SNL* characters into full-length films. Who knows. But back in the day, we were just trying to struggle to stay alive, so we didn't think of that stuff.

Ebony and Ivory (Part Two)

Many other sketches involved Eddie and me pairing together, like when we played Frank Sinatra and Stevie Wonder in a sketch where we modified "Ebony and Ivory," the hit song that had just come out by Paul McCartney and Wonder. Eddie and I were riffing at the piano with it one day during a writing session and got the idea for the sketch. We took it to our go-to writers, Barry Blaustein and David Sheffield, and they delivered a script. I don't remember anything specific about the original script they gave us, but the Sinatra part was a bit too edgy for me. Look, I know I got myself a reputation for protecting Mr. S. (and I'll talk about that more later), but hey, what are you going to do? I just thought we could make it funny *and* respectful.

The sketch has my Frank Sinatra and Eddie's Stevie Wonder together in a practice studio, talking about music and singing, with Wonder playing the piano. Mr. S. is looking to stay musically relevant with the "young people," and looks to partner with Wonder. Even so, he can't hide his old-school way of thinking entirely.

> **Frank Sinatra:** *Thank you, Stevie. I feel the same. I am very much into that tune you do with the Beatle kid—uh, what's his name? The one that looks like a broad?*
>
> **Stevie Wonder:** *His name is Paul McCartney, Frank.*

Frank Sinatra: *Yeah, yeah, yeah, that's the dude. Uh, would you be so kind as to run down that song for me, Stevie? Please?*

When Eddie starts singing the opening to "Ebony and Ivory" in the fashion of Wonder, the *SNL* audience breaks into loud applause. Because Eddie didn't just do a great impersonation of the singer—he actually sang very well.

Stevie Wonder: *Alright.*
Ebony and Ivory
live together in perfect harmony
Side by side on my . . .

Frank Sinatra: *Stevie, Stevie, hold it, Stevie. Now, something tells me that this is more than a song about playing the piano.*

Stevie Wonder: *Uh Frank, uh, it's about racial equality and unity of all people.*

Frank Sinatra: *Well, uh . . . I don't understand. When I think of Ebony, I think of a magazine that most people do not buy. And when I think of Ivory, I think of a soap that floats.*

Stevie Wonder: *Ebony and Ivory are the black and white keys on the piano, Frank.*

Frank Sinatra: *Alright, Stevie, I know that. You know that. But it's too artsy for the public—capiche? Now, I talked to the master, Sammy Kahn. Now, Sammy is a marvelous, marvelous songwriter—no offense, Stevie. And, uh. Sammy thinks we should go with something like Chocolate and Vanilla. Or, how about this: "Life is an Eskimo Pie, why don't we take a bite?"*

Stevie Wonder: *I'm afraid that might be a bit offensive to some people.*

Frank Sinatra: *Hey, who cares what the Eskimos think—they don't buy records, huh? OK, Stevie . . . let's see . . . Ebony and Ivory, huh? Ebony and Ivory. Hey, Stevie, what the hell are we beating around the bush for? This is 1982. Let's get right to the point! Huh? Hey, take it from the top. Swing it, Stevie! With a bounce, baby!*

Sitting down on the piano bench to Eddie's right, I put my left arm around his shoulder as he acted like he was playing the piano. We began to sing.

Frank Sinatra: *You are black, and I am white*
Life's an Eskimo Pie, let's take a bite!
That was groovy thinkin', Lincoln,
when you set them free.
We all know
Cats are the same
Maine to Mexico.
Good. Bad. Guys and chicks!

Stevie Wonder: *I am dark, and you are light.*

Frank Sinatra: *You are blind as a bat,*
and I have sight!
Side by side, you are my amigo, Negro,
let's not fight!

Stevie Wonder: *Ebony, ivory*
Living in perfect harmony.

Frank Sinatra: *We're talking Salt and pepper,*
Sammy and Dean
Stevie and me are peachy keen!

Stevie Wonder: *You are white.*

Frank Sinatra: *You are black—and who cares!*
Who cares, baby!

That's got to be one of my favorite sketches I did while on *SNL*. And not to get on a soapbox, but I have to wonder if we could even do a sketch like that on *SNL* today, given how political correctness has been ruining comedy for a decade or two now.

As I wrote this chapter, my old comedy club colleague Jerry Seinfeld got into heat with folks when he said, "The extreme left and PC crap and people worrying so much about offending other people . . . That's the end of your comedy."

Even my friend Bill Maher—who is certainly not a conservative—told *The New York Times*, "Comedians are afraid to make jokes in clubs, because somebody will tape it and send it out on Twitter and get the mob after you." Maher continues, "P.C. people protect feelings. They don't *do* anything. They're pointing at other people who are somehow falling short of their standards, which could have changed three weeks ago. They're constantly moving the goalposts so they can go, 'Gotcha!'"[15]

Eddie and I came years before political correctness or cancel culture. And *SNL* hasn't always gotten it right—myself included. I think you're doing good when you have the courage to offend both the left and the right—to go after your own "team" as much as you do the "other side." Equal opportunity offense.

Solomon and Pudge

In another example of a sketch involving me, Eddie, and a piano (yet very different in tone from the Sinatra-Wonder bit), we debuted "Solomon and Pudge" in January 1981. When people ask me what my favorite sketches were—which ones I am most proud of—I always say they were the Solomon and Pudge sketches. Let me explain.

The sketch came out of Eddie's imagination. We needed material—always had to come up with new material.

"Why don't we play two street guys in an old bar," I remember Eddie saying. He was thinking about guys he knew.

So we play these two old guys in a neighborhood bar, talking, laughing, and being friends. I'm Pudge, a grizzled piano-playing man who works in a bar for tips. Eddie is Solomon, a bar patron with sharp wit and ongoing troubles.

"You be Pudge, and I'll be Solomon," Eddie says. "And I'll pontificate. We'll just ad-lib it and improvise it."

"OK," I say. "I'll play the piano and put a black tooth in to make it look like I'm old and missing a few. And I'll be like an old jazz cat."

I remember John Madden was to host the show, and we told the producers about our sketch idea. Since it had an ad-lib element to it, they put the bit at the very end of the night because that way, it could go longer or shorter depending on how much time we had left in the show.

They staged the tavern in an area of the studio known as "Toscanini Corner." Back in the day when NBC had radio and they broadcasted symphony orchestra music, the great Italian conductor Arturo Toscanini would take his elevator up into that corner. Over the years since he retired in the 1950s, that corner became known as the place where sketches went to die—nothing worked well in that spot. People said it was because of Toscanini's ghost.

So "Solomon and Pudge" was stuck at the very end of the show and in that awful corner. But we nailed it. We ad-libbed virtually the whole thing. Eddie would riff, and I'd respond. He would tell stories, and I would follow—back and forth. The catchphrase we kept coming back to was, "You're crazy, man. Crazy."

There's always something bittersweet going on in the dialogue as Solomon loses his job or remembers his late wife. It doesn't sound like an *SNL* sketch. But that's what made it special for me—and the audience.

It was my job to get us out of the sketch—to land it. Eddie could get rolling with the riff, and I had to get him back on because Joe Dicso, the stage manager, would be signaling me, "Come on, you got to go. You got to go." Meaning that time was up, and the show was ending.

We didn't end on a joke. We ended with the catchphrase and a bit of melancholy or the realization that these men were bonded together. Then the lights dissolved out.

Boom. The audience went "wow"—and that was it. It was the best thing we did together. It was meaningful *and* funny.

Current *SNL* star Michael Che told *GQ* that they were his favorite sketches because they "had a lot of heart. It was kind of a sweet thing about this old man who was always down on his luck who had a really good sense of humor, and Joe Piscopo played a piano player at a bar."[16]

We reprised Solomon and Pudge five more times over that season and the next. Less script and more heart—that's what made Solomon and Pudge so organic. I always felt that it embodied the relationship between Eddie and me more than anything else.

It was crazy, man. Crazy.

13

ONE TOKE OVER THE
COCAINE LINE

I often hung out with Eddie in those early years and had a lot of crazy fun. But we never ever did any drugs. No joints, no pills—nothing. It was the 1980s, but even with all those lines of cocaine that seemed to be everywhere in those days—especially among entertainers and athletes—my large schnoz never got near 'em. Not a gram. Though I'm no choir boy, I've never done drugs—not even steroids during my muscle man years. In high school, I didn't like pot.

I have an obsessive-compulsive personality and am a bit of a hypochondriac, so I never tried drugs; I knew from others' experiences if you start it, you can't stop. On Sundays, I would drink—too much. Sunday was the only day off of the show, so I'd get the scotch out and sometimes get slammed: "Hey, it's Sunday," was my thinking. But never during the workweek—and never drugs.

The stories about drug use and drug-related jokes in the early days of *SNL* have been documented by many others. But that drug culture seemed to change under the new producers, Jean and Dick. Of course, I'm sure stuff still got smoked and ingested during my time there.

After they fired everyone except Eddie and me, Dick brought back in Michael O'Donoghue, one of Lorne's brilliant writer-producer guys, for the 1981–1982 season. Michael was a renegade, hippie, counter-culture maniac.

There definitely was a power imbalance between the producers and the cast, and especially so with someone like O'Donoghue. He was a decade older than me—two decades older than Eddie—and had written for the show's original cast for the first five years. He even acted in sketches and spoke the very first lines of the very first *SNL* show. He's the guy who spray painted "DANGER" on the wall of his office on his first day back—to remind everyone that "danger" was the missing ingredient from the previous season's *SNL*.

One day early in the season, Michael calls me into his office.

"Piscopo! I don't get what you do," he says with a tone of indifference. I'm not sure he was even looking up at me.

Just like that. This is what I'd get.

So I go, "Oh, I'm sorry, Mr. O'Donoghue. I'll try to do better." I know not to attack him back.

He goes, "Yeah. What *do* you do?"

I say, "Michael, honestly, I don't know what I'm doing here. I don't belong in the show. This is Danny Aykroyd's show. This is John Belushi's show. I'm not talented like that."

Then we talk more, and he goes, "Well, that Sinatra thing, yeah, that's pretty good. That Sinatra thing you do is pretty good. I like that."

OK, Michael likes my Sinatra. That's a start.

If you didn't write for yourself on *SNL*, you virtually were not on the air.

Getting your material on the air was a whole 'nother ball game. Getting to read-through each week was daunting. We had to come up with the sketch ideas, write them, and then pitch them to a mid-level producer. In this particular case, the producer was the biggest druggie on the planet.

I have always been against drugs, and I've never even tried cocaine. Pot, to me, is a brain killer. But because this guy did so many drugs simultaneously and was still able to function, I had immense respect for him.

Week after week, we would have to go before this stoned, bleary-eyed hippie-turned-accidental-producer, script in hand, and pitch our bits to him in his office.

He would sit at his desk, and you would sit in a chair on the other side, facing him.

As you went into your riff, our producer guy would take a Bic pen out of his pocket. The pen had no ink and no ballpoint filler in it.

Next, he would take a clear packet out of his shirt pocket. He would carefully tear open the top of the packet and pour out its white contents in lines on his desk.

As you would struggle not to watch (too much) and continue your sell, he would stick the pen up his nose and snort—very loudly by the way—the cocaine through the Bic pen.

Just as you're about to close out your pitch, Mr. Druggie-Producer-Person reaches back into his pocket and pulls out a joint. And fires it up right there at NBC.

At that point, you finished this fantastic idea for that week's show. And proudly look at this guy for approval.

Invariably, every week, he would take an enormous hit of the joint, hold it in for too long, and as he finally—and equally as long—exhaled, in a raspy voice, would proclaim, "That's not funny."

The Blues Brothers

Once Dick became the producer, members of the original cast began showing up at the studio. First of all, Billy Murray came in to host the show. He mentored us in a beautiful way—we were thankful for that.

Then John Belushi and Danny Aykroyd started coming in—not to host but just to hang out during rehearsal. Those of us *SNL* cast members who weren't part of the original group—those who weren't hired by Lorne—were always looked down on. Like unwanted step-children. But we never got that from Danny or John.

They admired Eddie immediately. The rest of us didn't have the star quality Eddie had, but we did our thing as the journeymen actors the show needed us to be.

Little by little, John saw me do some impersonations and sketches and he'd jump in there with input.

"Let me show you," he'd say and start acting out sketches for us—to help us, never to show us up or put on airs. Never.

One night, after a show wrapped up, John and Danny invited us to a hole-in-the-wall blues bar they owned on the corner of Green-wich and Warren down in the Village, to hang with them and members of the original cast.

So I'm there and just thinking, *Wow! This is amazing.* But I'm also a bit scared out of my mind. Gilda Radner is there. All the *SNL* icons and lots of famous people are there, as well as the more ordinary people like me. I'm just trying to keep to myself and not be a dork.

"Piscopo, come here," John says. I go over to him at the jukebox. He puts quarters into the machine and selects a song.

It's Sinatra's "New York."

John and I "start spreading the news" in unison. And in the chorus, we're dueling the "New York, New York" lines at each other.

I'm thinking, *This is unbelievable.*

We're just enjoying the song together. Neither of us is performing for anyone. We're not trying to be funny for a paycheck or the laugh of the crowd. It's just John and me off in the corner.

Until it isn't.

"Hey, look, John's with Piscopo doing Sinatra," someone shouts.

Everyone starts to come toward us. They see it's a moment—something they don't want to miss out on being part of as spectators. It's like they're saying, "Hey look, Belushi's doing something funny," when the poor guy just wants a private moment with the new kid.

John gets so uncomfortable that he just fades out of the scene, his smile replaced by a look that tells me this kind of thing always happens to him.

Isn't that sad? I felt bad for him. He couldn't walk around in public without being "John Belushi," with all the weight that carried.

I'll never forget that. He was a sweetheart.

———

A few months later, on March 5, 1982, I was down in Florida with The Fatman, Big Dave, my lifelong friend.

The phone rang. It was somebody from the show.

"Joe, I just want you to know that John Belushi died."

I just couldn't believe he was gone.

SNL wouldn't have lasted the fifty years it has if John hadn't been part of its family for the first five. He fueled the success of *SNL* even as the copious amounts of drugs he took fueled his performances.

And unfortunately for John—and for all of us who have missed him over the past four decades—that fuel eventually took him one step over the line of mortality.

———

All of us in the current *SNL* cast went to the Cathedral of St. John the Divine in New York to pay our respects to John.

The church was filled with family and a "who's who" of celebrities in mourning. His brother Jim—who joined the *SNL* cast the next season—eulogized his older brother: "John had something to give to everyone. He even had something to give to reporters, who are still getting something, it seems."

He was talking about how the news wouldn't stop rehashing the drug overdose details of John's premature death. The nation was beginning to awaken to the awful cost of drug addiction, which had been taken so lightly during the 1970s.

SNL had undoubtedly played its part in mainstreaming the drug culture of the seventies with sketches making light of lighting up and shooting up. Even after John's death, I did a Sports Guy sketch in 1983 called "Talking Dopeball," where we changed the words to "Talking Baseball" as a way of satirizing the rampant use of cocaine in Major League Baseball. That's the tricky thing about satire and comedy: Even when you parody a thing, you also end up promoting it.

Ironically, First Lady Nancy Reagan first used the now-famous phrase "Just say no" that same spring in response to an elementary student in Oakland asking her what she should do if someone offered her drugs. And though unrelated to John's death, a few weeks after his funeral, Nancy Reagan hosted a conference on drug abuse at the White House.

Danny gave the most memorable eulogy at John's funeral, telling us how he and John promised each other that whoever didn't die first would play a song by the Ventures at the other's funeral. So Danny pulled out a tape player and held it up to the microphone: "The 2,000-Pound Bee."

"John, this is for you," he said. He played the whole thing. We cried. It was wonderful.

———————

I'll tell you what. Everybody at *SNL* stopped doing drugs around that time. Maybe it was health-nut Jean's influence that began the trend. Maybe it was that Dick "No Drugs" Ebersol isn't Lorne Michaels. Whatever.

The end of the story is that when John Belushi died, rest his soul, everybody stopped. They all cleaned themselves up—or, at least, the culture changed in the offices and studio.

If drugs killed the great Belushi, who else would it claim?

14

MR. SINATRA

Frank Sinatra. I can't imagine how my life and career trajectory would be different if not for his influence. A fellow New Jersey, I felt the significance of Ol' Blue Eyes every time I got my hair cut. On the barbershop wall hung two framed pictures: the pope and Francis Albert Sinatra. And Mr. Sinatra's photo hung *above* that of the Holy Father.

Every week I broadcast a live *Sundays with Sinatra* from the power station WABC here in New York, playing two hours of Sinatra classics and giving historical context about the man and his music. And when I do my live entertainment shows, I always sing several Sinatra standards.

But the thing with Mr. Sinatra and me isn't mere admiration for a gifted entertainer. It goes deeper than our shared New Jersey and Italian roots. My love for Frank Sinatra is really about my dad and his generation. Mr. S. and my dad were born four months apart and are so similar in how they talked and laughed and operated. With my dad being a lawyer, you might find that hard to believe, but it's true.

So, when I connected with Mr. S., it was like another connection with my father.

The Letter

I remember when I first started to develop my impersonation of Mr. Sinatra while working in the comedy clubs. I would record him from TV onto a VHS tape, and then I'd record just the audio onto a cassette tape. Between the video and the audio recordings, I had my source material for studying his mannerisms and rhythms for how he talked and sang. The singing voice I got easily because I just felt that instinctively. But how to talk like Mr. S.—that took more practice.

I'd drive around in my Ford Fairmont, listening to the cassette and repeating it over and over. And I studied the video relentlessly and obsessively. When you do that, you just start to catch it or you don't, you know? It was trial and error.

Of course, Sinatra's accent was Hoboken—a North Jersey Italian accent—which is distinct from the rest of Jersey and very similar to mine. I would loosen it up a bit and make it a little more "street." If you go to North Jersey, coffee is *cawffee*—that kind of thing. There are times when I hear Mr. S. fall into that North Jersey accent where he roughed it up—so I'd do that too.

So, I was doing Sinatra at The Improv. I did a "The Lady Is a Tramp" bit where I kept repeating the end verse—the kind of humor Andy Kaufman would do. I just kept singing, "That's why the lady, that's why the lady, that's why the lady," and never ended it. It got laughs and I was honing my Sinatra impression with each night's performance.

Then I go to audition for *SNL* and do a Frank Sinatra impression, but this time it was crooning, "I don't stand the ghost of a chance . . . with you."

I did the whole thing, and they loved it and hired me. Which meant, of course, that they were going to want me to do the Sinatra impression on the show. But I was afraid to. I mean, I didn't want to do it because of respect for Mr. S.

But they said, "You got to do this. We need it, Joe."

The pressure was on.

So, I said, "OK, but I'm writing him a letter first."

I figured that somebody at NBC would tip him off anyway. Someone would tell Mr. Sinatra that this young punk on that Saturday night comedy show was going to impersonate him. I knew that Sinatra was very close with Dave Tebet, who was at the end of a long career as being head of talent at NBC when I was just coming on board with *SNL*. The entertainment world is small, and people talk.

I wrote a letter to Sinatra before I did the impersonation on the show for the first time and laid out the case for getting Frank's blessing. It went something like this: "Mr. Sinatra, I send this with the greatest of respect. You're my hero. Like my father is my hero. He told me you're the number one entertainer of all time. I mean no offense when I do the impersonations. They're done with complete respect first and foremost. If you find them to be offensive in any way, I'll cease and desist immediately."

I sent it to his lawyer Mickey Rudin. I don't even know how I got the address. I waited to hear back but never heard anything.

And so, I debuted my Mr. Sinatra. It was in a sketch where Charles Rocket played Ronald Reagan and Gail Matthius played Nancy Reagan. The joke was that Mr. Sinatra lobbied for Nancy to become the vice president. Ironically, during my four years on the show, I would go on to do President Reagan fourteen times.

Like I said, early on the *SNL* bosses just told me, "You got to do it, Joe. You got to do it." And they meant it.

I did it, OK, but then I took possession of the character myself. I said, "I have to be more protective of this." I just wanted to treat the Frank Sinatra character with more respect. We had fun. We laughed. But I always oversaw all the sketches.

I did Mr. Sinatra twelve times on *SNL* and a thirteenth time in 2015 for the fortieth anniversary show, in addition to forty-plus years of doing the impersonation on other shows. Mr. S. never sent word for me to "cease and desist." I never heard from anyone.

Well, that's not totally true. I never heard from anyone from Mr. Sinatra's camp telling me to *stop*, but I did eventually hear that the Chairman of the Board himself *approved* of what I was doing.

Charlie Callas, the very oddball-funny guy who often opened for the old man, was downstairs with him one Saturday night at Caesar's Palace. They were together in the dressing room and it was like 11:35 p.m. The TV was on in the background, and I came onto the screen—as Frank Sinatra.

Everybody stopped and there was dead silence in the room as Mr. S. watched it.

After the sketch ended, Charlie Callis said to Mr. Sinatra, "What do you think, captain?"

Frank said with a smile and a smirk, "He's pretty good." Then a pause before he added, "The little prick."

Frank Sinatra and Count Basie at Rehearsal

"Hey Joe. You know Frank Sinatra is playing at Radio City Music Hall with Count Basie on Sunday?" an NBC security guard said to me. Even early on at *SNL*, my admiration of Ol' Blue Eyes was a well-established fact around 30 Rock, and I considered Count Basie to be one of the greatest jazz artists ever, noted mostly for the impeccable synchronization and power of his "Count Basie Orchestra."

"I know, man, but I can't get tickets," I said.

"Well, you want to watch him rehearse?"

"You could get me that?"

"He'll be rehearsing in this building—of course I can," he said, dangling a set of keys. "I'll take you down there, and I'll sneak you in."

"You'll do that?"

"Yeah, but he's doing a three o'clock rehearsal, and he's so punctual, so don't be late."

So, on Tuesday I'm in my office and the security guard shows up and takes me downstairs. We walk down the hallway of the third floor, and he kicks open a secret door that I had not ever seen in all my times walking by that area.

"Go right through there."

I go in, and the door shuts behind me. I turn around to thank him, but he's gone.

It's the studio for *The Today Show*, but there are no cameras, no audience, no nothing. It's all empty except for a big Steinway grand piano in the center.

I'm thinking, *Ah, this is probably a* Candid Camera *joke on Joe. You guys are goofing on me.*

Then I hear rustling on the far side of the stage, and then . . . I see Frank Sinatra. His head is down reading a music chart, and he has a guy to his left.

Sid Mark, the original *Sundays with Sinatra* guy, was to his right.

Mr. S. starts to walk toward the piano. And I'm just hiding against the wall, man. I don't want to be seen, but I'm watching. I hear rustling at the door to my right, and Count Basie is brought into the studio in a wheelchair. He passed away about a year later, so this was near the end—but he still had it.

They wheel Count Basie in, and I hear Frank Sinatra say, "Hey, Bill, how you doing, baby?" Just like that. It was the thing. It was like—Sinatra, right there talking to Basie.

In pure jazz tones, Count Basie goes, "Hey, Francis, how you doing, man?"

I'm going like, *Oh my God, I can't believe I'm watching this.* Everything I dreamed of.

So then Mr. Sinatra walks up to the grand piano, and he lays the chart on the top of the piano. They wheel Count Basie up to the piano, and they start "Pennies from Heaven." I'm watching this, and Mr. S. is humming it. He's not singing it—they've done it a thousand times, but he wanted to get the riff going.

And that's when it happened.

All of a sudden Frank looked straight at me—still standing there in the darkness against the wall. Straight at me. He spotted me cold. And I froze, man.

I said, "Oh, now I'm in trouble."

With the music still playing, he turned his head, registered, tilted his head to the other side, blinked his eyes like he would do when he was staring at a person. Then he went right back to the music and let me be.

After that look from Frank, I snuck back out because I didn't want to be a pain in the neck.

I don't know how, but he never missed a trick. He was such a different human being, Frank Sinatra was. Once in a century do they come along like that—and he was that. He knew everything about his music and his business and the way he was going to live life. You couldn't mess with him, but he was also the nicest guy in the world. And he had instinct and talent like nobody else.

Friar's Club

The first time I actually met Frank Sinatra happened in 1984, when Dick Cavett walked me through the Friar's Club in New York.

At Mr. Sinatra's request, I came to be part of a "Dean Martin Roast"—this time with Dean Martin himself being the object of the roast because the club had named him "Man of the Year." I had my eyes down as Cavett walked and talked, but then I looked up, and about a foot away was Mr. Sinatra in the flesh. I couldn't help but get that butterflies feeling in my stomach. Again, it's the generational thing—meeting a hero who is like your dad.

Cavett says, "Joe Piscopo, Frank Sinatra." He wanted to make the introduction, right? I shook his hand, and he goes, "Hey, how are you?" Very nice and friendly. *Good*, I thought. Impressionists are not always appreciated by the people they impersonate. (Remind me to tell you about Andy Rooney.)

That night when I was on the dais, I looked down and saw Mr. Sinatra in the front row. I got more nervous than I ever remember being—even more than doing live TV in front of a national audience.

And since I'm the new kid in the Friars Club, Frank Sinatra introduces me to the room. I thought he was going to put me away, to put me in my place maybe for the *SNL* impressions. I thought he was going to go "this kid's a pain in the neck" or something like that. But he actually said, "This guy fractures me." Fractures! He used his great Sinatra word *fracture* to describe me. He complimented me up and down.

I thought that was so gracious and so wonderful. He didn't have to do that. I mean, this man is probably the most popular entertainer of all time and the big legend, and I mean, here's this Italian kid from New Jersey, doing an impression of him. In fact, I'm nearly making a living out of doing it. But he was just wonderful and gracious. And I'm telling you, it means a lot, because he is a hero. And I think I would've been hurt if it would've been otherwise.

Sinatra introduced me, saying, "He's got a lot of taste" and "You know, he does me—so he has got to be great." Then he says these lines: "And he's a good kid. He's Italian. He's like the vice chairman of the board: Joe Piscopo."

You're in a kind of tunnel when you're that young, and one of your heroes says your name—and christens you with a nickname that plays off his own. The hero I'd admired my whole life called me "the vice chairman of the board." I was like, *Wow.*

I went up to the microphone, with Mr. S. on my left, Dean Martin on my right, and all the big guns of show business on the dais and in the audience. I started right in with my impression. With the full Sinatra voice and diction, I said to him:

"You know, I like the way you say the word . . . *you.*"

The audience laughed at the impression.

"Like, *you* go: 'I don't stand'"—more laughter—"'a ghost of a chance with . . . *you.*'"

Sinatra sat there coolly, holding his Jack Daniels and cigarette with one hand, but he seemed to be enjoying it. I looked down at him, and he said, "That's pretty good. That's pretty good."

Here's this young punk taking on the legend and living to tell about it. I waited for the laughter to subside and went in for one more. "Can I call you Frank?"

Leaning into his mic and twinkling those blue eyes, Mr. Sinatra said with a staccato, "No."

The room roared with laughter.

He got the biggest laugh from that simple and curt "No" because it was like, "All right kid, you're funny, but don't mess with me. I got you."

That's how I met Mr. Sinatra, and by the grace of God, it was a love affair ever since.

———

In 1990 I was a guest of Mr. Sinatra for his seventy-fifth birthday. His guests met up at the Waldorf Hotel, shuttled over to the Meadowlands, and then returned to the Waldorf. I sat with Sonny Burke, his longtime producer. I was just a fly on the wall, nobody of any true importance that night. But we spent the night and celebrated his birthday in a room of celebrities and friends of Sinatra. It was amazing.

Afterward, we all lined up to say goodbye to him. He was casual at that point, open-collar like my father would have been with friends. I pulled together my best goodbye line and said, "Mr. Sinatra, what a distinct honor to be here, sir."

He leaned into me, pulled me closer, and spoke with that generous smile, "Ah, I had a better time than anybody."

Just like that. That's exactly what my father would have said.

And that's the attachment to my dad. They walked the same and were gracious and classy in much the same way.

And as I said, they were close in age. Almost exactly the same age. Mr. S. was born in 1915 and Pop was born in April 1916. About four months apart, and they had the same exact upbringing.

That generation, man—God bless them—I miss that. It's all about history and heritage and how you can't forget where you're from.

———

When people ask me which impression I enjoy doing the most, of the dozens and dozens I've performed over the decades, without a doubt it's Sinatra because I like to think I channel Frank. I don't "do" him so much as I just kind of channel the greatness of Mr. Sinatra. There are times where I'm onstage, and I can feel the old man. I can just feel the whole presence of Frank Sinatra, and then I can execute it vocally. I don't know where that comes from, but that's what I enjoy doing best. His music is great, of course, and I love being onstage playing any kind of music—but especially Sinatra's tunes.

Paul Shaffer was the one who originally told me to "take this Frank Sinatra thing on the road." He gave me that advice in 1981 when I debuted my Sinatra on *SNL*.

I said, "What do you mean?"

"Get a band and hit the road with it," Shaffer said. And he introduced me to Ralph Schuckett, who did all the arrangements and conducted the orchestra.

I took it down to Caesar's in Atlantic City. I had no idea what I was doing. They wanted to pay me way too much money, like $125 grand for a couple of shows—and this was in the 1980s.

Whoa, OK, I'll do this. I'll do this bit, I thought.

So I went and did my best. I've continued to do these shows over the years, and they've melded into a pretty hip, cool, retro-style show now. And Shaffer was the guy who gave me the original idea.

————————

Years later, I was with Tommy Dreesen, my buddy and the comic genius who opened for Mr. Sinatra in Vegas. We saw him down the hall, and Tommy insisted we go over and say hi.

Tommy said, "Hey, Frank, you know Joe Piscopo?"

And Mr. S. goes, "Do I know Joe Piscopo? I know him better than his father knows him. I know him longer than his father knows him."

Tipping the hat to my old man. That was classy.

15

UNDER PRESSURE

SNL Season 8 | 1982–1983

Julia Louis-Dreyfus, Brad Hall, and Gary Kroeger joined the cast for the show's eighth season, all coming to *SNL* from the Practical Theater Company in Chicago. Even though they were young (Julia was just twenty-one), they brought with them a lot of experience and chemistry (Brad and Julia eventually even got married).

Dick brought those kids in from Chicago, and they were great right from the start. Looking back now, I feel guilty for never stepping into their offices and asking, "Hey, what can we do to help you guys?" They crushed it anyway, so they didn't need my help to succeed. But years later in an interview with Stephen Colbert, Julia described her *SNL* time as "a pretty brutal time" and complained about sexism and drug use on the set.

During her final season on *SNL* (1984–1985), Julia worked alongside writer Larry David, who was still pretty much unknown and shared with her in the misery of working for the show. A few years later, of course, Larry cocreated *Seinfeld* with Jerry—and they hired Julia for her now legendary Elaine Benes role.

Julia said her *SNL* experience installed a "fun meter" into her: "I learned I wasn't going to do any more of this show business crap unless it was fun."[17]

Was *I* having fun? Yes and no.

The season opened in late September 1982 with Chevy Chase hosting, and for the musical act we landed Queen. Freddie Mercury's voice was shot from touring, but he belted out "Crazy Little Thing" and "Under Pressure." Unbeknownst to anyone that night, this would be Queen's final time performing in the US with Freddie in the lead.

As it was my third season on *Saturday Night Live*, I should have felt calm and cool like the veteran I had become. After all, I had been part of nearly two hundred sketches in two years (including voice-overs). I averaged five sketches per show, so I wasn't exactly a rookie.

But I felt under pressure a lot of the time. Coming up with new material every week was as daunting a task as I ever encountered. Remember, if you didn't write for yourself, you wouldn't get on the air much. I thought through my own life experiences to find material, which is how my effeminate high school drama teacher came to be "Mr. Blunt" in a sketch that season. But there's only so much of that you can draw from before the well runs dry.

I can remember Eddie and me staying up all night trying to come up with new material. We were like two college roommates cramming for a final—we both got punchy and started riffing, and some of the best stuff came out of that. Those are good memories.

That season I debuted impersonations of Phil Donahue, Ed McMahon, and other celebrities, including Joan Rivers. When she hosted the show that season, we did a "Dueling Joans" sketch together—with me in drag. She said I looked like Joan Rivers on steroids. In fun, I called her a name I won't print here. It was great.

One of the most memorable sketches I did that year had me impersonating both President Reagan and Jerry Lewis—in the same sketch. It began with me as Reagan, sitting at a desk addressing the nation. I'd say a few sentences and then the camera would show an economic chart. And when the camera came back on me, my character slowly turned into Jerry Lewis—as the nutty professor. I had the teeth in hand and a comb to mess up my hair from Reagan to Lewis.

I knew every beat that I was going to do and had it all worked out—don't forget, this is live TV, so you get only one shot at it.

And here's what I remember most. After I finished the sketch and we went to the commercial, I overheard a member of the stage crew who had been around for years, talking softly to another crew member.

"This guy," he said, pointing at me, "this is Aykroyd."

Like that. Wow. It was a compliment. And when the *crew* compliments you—man, that's when you know you're doing OK. So that made me feel really good.

Eddie and I teamed up that season for half of the one hundred sketches he took part in. Sometimes it was for a one-off sketch, like when we played astronauts in the space shuttle. Sitting side-by-side in close quarters, Eddie's character revealed his love for me—yes, that kind of love.

A recurrent sketch that debuted that season was "Dion's Hairstyling," where we play two flamboyant beauticians, Dion and Blair. This was in the early 1980s, so we had a lot of fun with it in ways that you might not get away with nowadays.

That fall was the final few months that Eddie wasn't a household name. His first film, *48 Hours*, released in December 1982. That was the first of seven films in a row that went number one at the box office for Eddie. What an incredible run.

Eddie even hosted *SNL* the week of the movie's release when his costar Nick Nolte partied too hard and called Dick to cancel out on being our host. Nobody had ever been the host of the show while also a cast member—and nobody has done it since. At the end of the cold open, he turned to the camera and shouted, "Live from New York, it's the Eddie Murphy show!"

16

MERRY OLD SOULS

SNL Season 9 | 1983–1984

As I began my fourth season on *SNL* in the fall of 1983, I didn't know it would be my swan song. Eddie was on his way out—everyone at *SNL* knew that. He even had a special contract with Dick Ebersol that season, allowing him to take part in only half the shows and to film a bunch of sketches with the cast that would be dispersed throughout the season. You couldn't keep a star like that at the show forever when Hollywood was offering him $10–20 million per movie. Eddie and I solidified our relationship even more, so I began to contemplate my own departure from *SNL*. After all, we came in together, so maybe we should walk out together.

I felt very much like I was in my wheelhouse that season. I had just shot the film *Johnny Dangerously* with Michael Keaton and felt confident in where my career seemed to be heading. (This wasn't my first movie, but we'll get to that later.) Doing the show had become fun too. And clearly, I was the veteran and "old guy" of the cast.

I'm an old soul. If you've caught anything about me so far in this book, it's that my entertainment values have always run toward the generations that came before me. The music, the laughs, the shows—I take energy from the old stuff and the way the old guys and gals did their work long before I hit the stage.

So the 1983–1984 season brought a lot of joy to me personally because, more than any other season I was on *SNL*, Dick Ebersol got us "old souls" as hosts. Many of them were the old guard from yesteryear who still had a fire in their entertainment engine: Jerry Lewis, Flip Wilson, the Smothers Brothers, and Don Rickles. We even had old guy hosts from outside comedy like former NYC Mayor Ed Koch; former Senator George McGovern, who had run for president against Nixon when I was in college; and veteran newscaster Edwin Newman, finishing his twenty-three-year career with NBC that year.

I was so happy to see all these guys jump into hosting *SNL* because the show had not been warmly received by all the greats from the older generation. I don't mean any disrespect when I say that because everyone is entitled to their opinion.

I had a chance to talk with Bob Hope once when a friend, his eye doctor, put me on the phone with him. It didn't go well, though, because it seemed he wasn't a fan of *SNL*.

Jackie Gleason didn't like the show either, from what I heard, which was a disappointment because Mr. Gleason was a hero of mine. Eddie and I did *Honeymooners* sketches on *SNL* (Eddie played an awesome version of Art Carney's character, Ed Norton). And we created "The Honeymooners Rap" together, a fun, silly song that was received well and was played at dance clubs across the country. We wanted to do a video of the song, but Gleason—or his people—wouldn't grant us the rights to do any *Honeymooners* footage because he didn't think it was funny. From what I understand, they thought we were too edgy.

Jerry Lewis

But you know who did love us? The one and only Jerry Lewis.

Jerry agreed to host the November 19, 1983, show and went all in on getting prepared, just like any other host would do. I remember well his arrival in the offices because it was the first time I ever met him.

We get the word from security: "Jerry Lewis is coming up the elevators now."

So I leave my office on the seventeenth floor and head down the hallway in that direction. When I hear the elevator door open and him talking, in my best impersonation of his famous character voice—that blend of annoying and loud, I yell out,

"Jerry! Hey Jerry! Jerry!"

That's when I hear back, in the same voice, "Joe?"

"Jerry?!" I shout in response.

"Joe!"

"Jerry!"

He grabs me into a big hug, and it's an immediate love fest. Two generations enjoying genuine camaraderie.

That week was the greatest. He knew I admired him and had been doing impersonations of him, so he came into the building prepared to work hard but also to begin a friendship with me.

I sat next to him while he read through the scripts.

With the sketches, I said, "Let me do you to you." And I did Lewis to Lewis—and then Eddie came into the sketch, also doing Jerry. You can see this online, the three of us all impersonating Jerry—it was great.

Probably our best sketch of the night had Jerry in a hospital bed for a major surgery. I played Dean Martin as the surgeon who was about to operate on him but was smoking a cigarette, drinking a martini, and ogling the dolled-up nurses. The real Dean Martin saw and loved the sketch, which led to that invite to the Friar's Club Roast I discussed earlier.

What's hilarious to remember is how Eddie and I watched the original *Nutty Professor* starring Lewis to get prepped for that week. Eddie didn't really know about the legacy of Jerry then—at least not on the personal level that I did, having grown up watching all the Lewis movies.

Of course, Eddie went on to do his own version of these movies with the whole Klump franchise. This is hilarious to me because, when we were on *SNL*, Eddie didn't like putting on much makeup or prosthetics for sketches—not at all. As I mentioned earlier, I broke him into it for his "older Muhammad Ali" impersonation. With the Klump movies, he went all in on the special effects to great success.

I learned a lot from Jerry Lewis, an old-school consummate entertainer. Jerry was really a true genius with physical comedy. Watch those early films like *The Nutty Professor* and *Cinderfella*. Very Chaplinesque.

Unless you're as glib as Seinfeld, you'd better not just stand there when you're onstage. You'd better keep dancing or gyrating because you have to keep the crowd interested in what you're doing. From watching the greats of the past who excelled in maintaining the crowd, you get a sense of how much physicality it takes to entertain.

And when you do an impression, you have to absorb the physical nature of the character. You channel your body into what their body does. Like when you do Frank Sinatra, you've got to feel your shoulders going back, to maintain the meticulous Sinatra-esque stature.

When I'm onstage, I like to do a lot of physical comedy and even physical music and instrumentation: guitar, saxophone, drums, and even the flute. The instrument becomes more than just a way to play music. When I play "Sing, Sing, Sing" on the drums, the physicality and unintentional flailing of my arms adds to the entertainment and humor.

Don Rickles

And speaking of physical humor, I'll never forget when Don Rickels hosted *SNL*. Incidentally, it was the same week Michael Jackson's hair caught on fire while filming a Pepsi commercial, and Steve Jobs launched the Mac computer with his famous "1984" commercial.

If you're a younger reader and don't know who I'm talking about—please Google "Don Rickles" and be ready to laugh. Oh, and your jaw will drop because you can't believe he got away with saying what he did. The times were different.

When Rickles hosted, we were nervous because Eddie wouldn't be there. That was part of those final few months when his contract allowed him to work on other projects away from the show. Eddie was busy shooting what would become his first *Beverly Hills Cop* blockbuster.

So Dick Ebersol comes to me and says, "Look, Eddie's not here. It's all up to you this week." If you're a baseball fan, Dick and I were like Billy Martin and Reggie Jackson—or Earl Weaver and Jim Palmer. The boss calls the shots and sets the tone—but that doesn't mean the players all enjoy the tone.

He says, "Look, it's up to you. You got to make this work." So the pressure is on—thanks, boss.

I cold open as President Reagan in the Oval Office doing an infomercial selling steak knives.

Then Rickles does his opening monologue and just kills it. He's hilarious and sets the tone for the night, right?

But then, backstage, Jimmy Belushi, Rickles, and I are about to go on to do our "Witness Protection" sketch. Jimmy and I are cops—Feds who are talking to Rickles's character about the witness protection program he's going into. That was the premise of the sketch we were about to do.

I hear the stage manager go, "We're live in one minute."

I look over at Rickles. He's sitting in his chair, but his arms are down at his side. He looks like he's worked up.

"Don, you're sweating profusely," I say.

Rickles looks up at me and says, "This sketch isn't going to work, Joe. It's not funny. It just doesn't work."

"Don, you just killed in the monologue," I say. "It's going to be fine."

"I don't know what to do with it," he says.

I don't know what to say, so I blurt out: "But you're Don Rickles. You're Don Rickles."

I just mean to remind him that he can make anything work. As if that fact is going to turn a poorly written sketch into comedy gold.

So now we're into the sketch and I'm giving a speech to Rickles's character. With a staccato speech pattern, I'm telling him one thing after another. "You gotta do this" and "You gotta do that" kind of lines. And with every word I say, I lightly slap him in the face.

Clearly, that isn't written into the script, a fact the live audience picks up on because of the surprised look on Rickles's face. The energy of the sketch begins to escalate, and Rickles doesn't miss a beat. He plays along with it like we had practiced this all week.

Then, knowing the cameras are behind me, I put my hand over his mouth—the camera can't see that. And I plant a kiss on what seems to be his lips.

The crowd roars.

I take the big funny cowboy hat he has on, turn it sideways, and drive it down on his head. Physical humor, like the Three Stooges. It's survival, baby—survival on live television. You do whatever it takes.

Rickles goes right into a pratfall, and boom!—we are off and running.

By the grace of God, I mean, we kill it. The whole show has energy. From that point on, Rickles arbitrarily says things in the middle of other sketches, breaking the fourth wall—like when he turns to my character and says, "Hey, I haven't forgotten how you slapped me around in that other sketch." Or when he says things you couldn't get away with now: "I'm going to send Eddie Murphy over to rob your house."

Oh my—did he just say that?

He did. Because he's Don Rickles.

At the night's end, Ebersol comes over and hugs me. "I love you, man. I love you," he says.

I was the utility guy. When Dick couldn't get a sketch to work, he knew I'd make it work. I wasn't the star, but I could get it done and make them laugh. Sweat a bit, and you'll figure it out—just don't let 'em down.

And I'm still in the blue collar of show business. Put some sweat into it and figure it out.

Don and I went on to become very, very close friends. Years later, I opened for him at Foxwoods, a Connecticut casino, and by God's grace, it worked out great.

The band was great. I did my music and comedy for about forty minutes. As I came off the stage, I was sweating. I was totally dripping wet from playing the drums, doing my bits, and doing my best—because I was with the legend. I got to really show myself that night. I felt great about my opening act. The crowd applauded and cheered as I walked off the stage.

There was a stairway to step off the stage, and Don was there with a drink in his hand. He looks up at me and says, "Joe, try to do better next time, will you?"

That's Rickles for you. He was a great guy. Much missed.

Worth a Nickel

Eddie's final time being live in the studio with us for a show was on February 25, 1984, *SNL*'s 173rd show. He didn't return to *SNL* for thirty-one years until he appeared in February 2015 for the fortieth anniversary special.

Though he wasn't even twenty-three yet, Eddie was a four-year veteran of *SNL* and had taken part in 279 sketches on the show. He had also filmed three movies during that time and was in the middle of his fourth.

Since I didn't have Hollywood movies pressuring my schedule to the same extent as Eddie, I hadn't missed a single one of the seventy-two *SNL* shows that aired since my hiring. During that time, I took part in 394 sketches, including ones for which I did voices. Eddie and I were partnered together on 154 of those sketches.

Nowadays, Eddie is in his early sixties and I'm still a decade older. By comparison, Don Rickles and Jerry Lewis were both fifty-eight when they hosted *SNL*. Nobody would now describe Eddie and me as the "fresh young faces" of anything, as they did when we were breaking in with *SNL*. Life travels by fast—and faster, it seems, every year.

So it's fitting that in our final sketch together, we played two really old guys sitting on a park bench talking about how everything used to cost "just a nickel"—even things that truly never cost a nickel, like a suit, a piano, a house, or a car. These two old men enjoyed the sentimental reminiscing, but they also just enjoyed each other's company.

When you watch that sketch online, you'll see that Eddie and I had so much fun with the lines and each other that we broke character.

"I read the card wrong," Eddie said, pointing to the cue cards being held just offstage.

That got laughs from the audience, so I ad-libbed by pointing at the poofy white hair wig and glasses I was wearing and saying, "Did you ever notice I look like Al Franken in fifty years?" Al had, of course, been part of the original *SNL* team and then returned as a writer and sometimes cast member from 1985 to 1995. I always liked Al and got along with him when he came around the show.

The stage manager motioned for us to end the skit, so Eddie said, "If we keep talking, it will mess up everything."

I laughed hard, and then I leaned over and laid my head on Eddie's shoulder. The cameras pulled back, and the sketch came to an end as the audience applauded.

And that was the end of the road for Eddie and me being on *SNL* together: two old souls sitting on a bench together having a good time.

————

My own *SNL* finale came five shows later, on May 12, 1984, when Dick Ebersol brought in five people as hosts, including Billy Crystal, who would join the cast the following year.

Billy and I did the cold open, with Billy in blackface as Sammy Davis Jr.—with Sammy's approval. (Did I mention that times were different?) I played the part of Mr. Sinatra one final time on the show (except, of course, when I reprised the part for *SNL*'s fortieth anniversary special in 2015).

For my final sketch as a cast member of *SNL*, I played Curly in a sketch where the Three Stooges taught a self-defense course. Dressed in martial arts clothing, I was bouncing and hopping and scooting around the stage on my butt, just like the original Curly would do. All of that was scripted.

What wasn't part of the script, however, was for my pants to come loose and drop to my ankles—not once, but twice.

Everyone broke character in laughter at Piscopo sans pants.

And that's how I ended my four-year run on *Saturday Night Live*.

17

EXITING DICK EBERSOL'S *SNL*

May 1984

W hy did I leave *SNL*?
        I can think of several reasons, which I'll explain here
because I need to correct the false ideas. There's this belief that I didn't
leave on my own terms and didn't get invited back for another season.
But that's simply not true.

I got a solid offer to return to the show for a fifth season, but I
turned it down. I earned $3,000 per episode for my first season on
SNL (1980–1981, 13 episodes, $39,000); then $15,000 per show for
the second season (1981–1982, 20 episodes, $300,000); $20,000 each
episode for the third season (1982–1983, 20 episodes, $400,000);
and $25,000 a show for my fourth season (1983–1984, 19 episodes,
$475,000).

Now, keep in mind these two economic facts from my last year at
SNL: In 1984, the annual median household income in the US was
$26,000, and Major League Baseball's minimum salary for rookies
was $40,000.

So here I was, earning more in one week than a family or a rookie baseball player would earn in a year. And remember, that's just the money I earned from *SNL*. The cash from commercials never stopped coming in, and multiple Hollywood movie pitches were showing up for my consideration.

So, for the record, I was offered a contract for a fifth season of $25,000 a week, but I turned it down.

———————

The reasons for my leaving *SNL* go like this:

First and foremost, once Eddie told me he was leaving—something he told me before the 1983–1984 season even began—I felt I didn't want to be there without him. We'd had a good run together.

As I've shown in the previous chapters, the *SNL* writers paired the two of us together in so many sketches that it just seemed like something was naturally coming to an end. I have no doubt that if Eddie had stayed, I would have too. But that's not the way things happened. I felt close to the other cast members, but it seemed like it would be the end of an era once he left.

———————

Another reason for my leaving is that the weekly schedule for doing a live TV sketch comedy show is very intense. I'm not the only cast member in the history of *SNL* to state this fact as a reason for leaving the show.

People ask me if there was a lot of pressure each week. You can't even imagine. Even today, when I go by NBC, I have anxiety. You didn't get into sketches if you didn't write for yourself. So you'd bust your chops to get material written, then do your dress rehearsal and hope the producers would accept your sketch.

Most of the time with Eddie and me, the stuff got on the air. But for me, at least, there was so much stress and pressure—and

I felt at the time that it would be a break to walk away from the pressure. When I think of the bad parts of working on the show, coming up with new material every week was as daunting a task as I ever encountered.

Another unpleasant task for *SNL* cast members is having to do a sketch that you *knew* wasn't really funny, but the show needed to fill time. You'd do it as best as you could, but the sketch would bomb. And then, on Sunday, I'd hear from all my boys back in Jersey, who would call me up and bust my chops for how terrible the sketch was.

———————

And then there was the Dick Ebersol factor. Was there tension between Dick and me? Yes.

But it's old news for me to say that Dick and I clashed often. Am I going to dish out the fresh dirt and throw folks under the bus for things that happened forty years ago? Sorry, but that's not my style.

Dick is a great producer who has worked on so many huge TV events across the spectrum, from sports, music, live events, drama, and comedy. His work stands on its own merits. That said, there will always be creative differences between cast and producers—especially when you work together on a show like *SNL*.

Dick and I had tension, but it wasn't only me. It was like the whole cast was pitted against the producers, who often came to us with an attitude like, "All right, here's the material for this week, whether you like it or not." There's always natural tension like this on any television show.

But we'd come out swinging because it was our job to make the material work—and our reputations were on the line if the show fell flat. Viewers at home don't think to blame the producer or writers. Blame just gets laid at the feet of the cast, no matter how lame the scripts handed to us were.

But honestly, Dick and I had one of those healthy relationships where, even though we didn't really agree creatively, we both knew the main goal was to do a good show. And that meant making people laugh. That said, the struggles I had with Dick contributed to me wanting to leave *SNL*.

But Dick Ebersol did make a direct offer to me for $25,000 a week to continue on the show as a cast member.

Beyond that, the late Brandon Tartikoff, whom I consider to be the brains of any project he was part of—and one of the most decent executives in the history of TV—brought me out to LA to discuss a unique offer. Over breakfast at the Polo Lounge, Brandon told me they were discussing using three or four people (Billy Crystal, me, and a few others) in rotation as permanent hosts for the show. They spun that idea around but ultimately stuck with having a fresh guest host every week as usual.

I would never leave the show if they needed me, but I knew they already had Jimmy Belushi as an anchor. And Billy Crystal, Christopher Guest, and Martin Short were all coming on board for the next season.

I remember thinking, *I don't need to be here. They've got this covered.*

And honestly, I *didn't* need to be there. They did do great.

––––––

I should have stayed longer, like Kenan Thompson, who has been there for over twenty years! OK, I couldn't have lasted that long, but look at Phil Hartman, the utility guy who came in after me. He had a solid eight-year run.

People have described those guys as glue for the rest of the cast. They're versatile players who make every scene better, even though they're not the main star in the sketch. That's what I was doing on *SNL*, and I should have stuck with it, picking up a nice, big paycheck every week.

But I didn't want to be there anymore.

Would I do the same thing if I had it to do over? Considering all the circumstances, I probably would.

———————

SNL gave me a career, so I always treat the show with the utmost respect it deserves. For my entire life since being on *SNL*, people come up to me to talk about the show. It opens doors of conversation and even opportunities for work.

When I attended the fortieth anniversary special, people came up to tell me how much they enjoyed the show while I was on the program.

I saw actor Bradley Cooper that night, and being a big fan of his work, I went up and told him so.

"Bradley, hi. Joe Piscopo. I'm a big fan."

Bradley gets up in my face, grabs me by my arms, and throws me against the wall. He shouts, "Joe f—king Piscopo! I know everything you've ever done, dude!"

"Whoa," is all I could say.

Then Paul Rudd came over. "Joe, man, you were my guy." Fred Armisen, Jay Pharoah, and many others did the same. It was the most humbling weekend.

So I have nothing but respect for the show. I'm grateful to those folks who gave me the opportunity to be on NBC. To all the producers and staff. To Jean Doumanian who hired Eddie and me. And certainly, to Lorne Michaels, who created the show and returned to lead it for another four decades—what a run!

I'm grateful because you can work in entertainment forever once you're on the show.

And when you look at the show today, I don't know how you'd even try to pick out one or two favorites from the current and recent cast because there has been so much incredible talent over the years. How do they keep restocking with such good talent? Aidy Bryant is as funny as anybody I've ever seen. Kate McKinnon is brilliant. I'm a big Pete Davidson fan. I like Colin Jost and Michael Che's delivery on Weekend Update. And the only criticism I'd made about Bowen Yang is that they don't use him enough.

My point is that we *SNL* cast members come and go, but the show goes on. We play our parts, work our butts off, utilize whatever talent we brought in the door with us, and hopefully get some luck thrown our way for good measure.

Part 4

JAMMIN' ME

1984–1990

18

DORK DAD & DIVORCE

O ne of my dearest old buddies is a guy I call "The Fatman." He's not so much fat as he is huge—six-foot-seven and could have been a linebacker for any NFL team.

Hanging with The Fatman is a book in itself, but I'm not the kind of guy to break loyalties.

Recently Big Dave reminded me that when I was a kid, I used to always tell him that I couldn't wait to be a father with children to take care of. And to this day, fatherhood is my single greatest joy.

I am a dork dad. I love my children, and I'm a really dedicated father. I take that very, very seriously. It's what it's all about, man.

I can't seem to hold on to my wives. That's my next book: *Too Many Wives, Not Enough Children.* But despite the fact that I can't seem to hold on to the mothers of my children, I always respect the fact that they were the people who carried these beautiful kids into the world and blessed me with the greatest gifts from God.

When my firstborn, Joey, was born in 1979, the Lamaze form of childbirth was all the rage. So his mom and I went to those classes that teach you things like how to breathe—and how the dad is supposed to bring a sandwich to the delivery because you might get hungry.

His mother was stoic and determined in delivery.

Me? I cried. I completely fell apart. The Lamaze thing had me at her head, wiping her brow with a sponge. I needed it more than she did to dry my tears.

To my pleasant surprise, immediately after delivery, the nurse handed me our 8 lb. 11.5 oz. handsome baby.

Joey, his mom, and I were fortunate to be in the delivery room when no one else was there. Just the three of us—father, mother, and newborn.

As I held Joey in my arms and looked directly into his eyes, I felt an incredible, intense, and instinctive love like I've never experienced before.

For years, Joey would go with me on the road. I would proudly bring him onstage as a special surprise in my show. He would kill 'em every time. A thick voice, an awesome stage presence, and a father-son act worth the price of admission alone. It was schmaltz at its best.

You either loved it or wanted to vomit.

I loved it. And I loved being with my flesh and blood on the road. We would laugh, watch bad TV while eating bad room service, and it was the best time I can remember on the road.

This was an incredibly difficult time in the lives of what once was a strong and loving family team.

My son and ex-wife asked that I not mention about this period of our lives. Out of love, I must respect their wishes. The important thing is that I'm still friends with Nancy.

Listen, if it wasn't for her, there would be no SNL for Joe. I wouldn't be in show business. Nancy was essential in everything in my career. I couldn't have done it without her. When I was just starting out and making basically pocket change, she went to work as a legal secretary and supported us. I was coming home in the middle of the night from the comedy clubs, and she was a rock of support.

And I have a forever strong, loving, and prideful bond with my son.

The reason for my existence is being a dad. It's the greatest privilege and blessing to be the father of my children.

———————

The reason for my existence is being a dad. It's the greatest privilege and blessing to be the father of my children.

19

HOLLYWOOD HITS &
ALMOST THERES

In the September 30, 1993, episode of *The Simpsons*, Homer said
this about me: "A maturing Joe Piscopo left *Saturday Night Live* to
conquer Hollywood."

That's sure what it seemed like I did from 1984 until some point
in the early 1990s. Television, movies, commercials, live events,
books, and music albums—I seemed to be firing on all cylinders in
the 1980s. After all, when you find *SNL* success, Hollywood (to use
that term in the broadest way to mean the entertainment business)
comes calling. Could I turn that interest into an entire career? That
was to be determined.

I think actor Owen Wilson was right when he said, "You can think
of Hollywood as high school: TV actors are freshmen. Comedy actors
are maybe juniors. And dramatic actors—they're the cool seniors." In
that sense, Hollywood saw me as a junior—a viable moneymaker for
them as a comedy actor. They put me to work, and I made my own
opportunities too.

"It's a perfect time to be a comedian," I explained to journalists at the time, "because there are so many outlets. With my films, if they don't work in the theaters, they work on video. With TV, if the networks don't want it, then take it to HBO. And I can even go back to the original form of doing live entertainment. I thrive on 'live'—and it's the most fun."

From *King Kong* to *Johnny Dangerously*

My film debut actually came several years before *SNL*. I bet you didn't know that I, Jeff Bridges, and the beautiful Jessica Lange teamed up for a 1976 summer blockbuster movie, the remaking of *King Kong*. Of course, that's like saying in 1962, Bob Eucker combined with his teammate Hank Aaron to hit forty-six home runs (Aaron hit forty-five of them).

When I was just starting out at The Improv, I sat talking to my friend Jimmy Brogan, a very funny guy who went on to be Jay Leno's head writer. We got word that the great Italian film producer Dino De Laurentiis was putting together this remake of the classic *King Kong* film. They needed extras down at the World Trade Center Plaza.

"Hey Jimmy, let's go get ourselves in *King Kong*," I said.

So we showed up for our big motion picture debut—us and the thirty thousand (literally) other extras who, on cue, ran and screamed in panic from the big gorilla in a climactic scene.

No matter how slow you watch the scene, you can't make me out. But hey, after investing only a few hours of my time, I got what I needed at the start of my career: a line on my résumé, baby!

———

When you're just getting started you take whatever you can get. And once you're established, you hope that nobody finds this earlier material. With the internet, of course, nothing ever dies.

For example: *American Tickler.*

This was a sketch comedy film I had a small part in. Released in 1977, it was just awful—a low-budget copycat of *National Lampoon* or *Kentucky Fried Theater* (and if someone describes your project as a cheap knockoff of something called *Kentucky Fried Theater*, you know you've sunk low).

I contributed to a few of its mostly unfunny scenes of stupidity. Why? I wanted to work in entertainment, and this was several years before *SNL*. And they *did* pay me.

I remember thinking, *Wow, I'm in a movie—and not just an extra!*

But you know what's funny is how once I broke big with *SNL*, the folks who produced the VHS tapes of *American Tickler* suddenly changed the cover art to show my face rather prominently. It was like, "Hey, we know we only gave that Joe fellow a few seconds in the movie, but he's famous now, so splash his funny mug on the box."

Everybody's got these kinds of projects in their closet. This was one of mine.

———

After *SNL* brought me out of obscurity, I began to make appearances on talk shows (David Letterman, Johnny Carson) and other TV shows like the 1982 version of *Battle of the Network Stars*—hosted by Howard Cosell. If you're too young to remember, this was an early form of unscripted reality TV where actors and actresses from CBS, NBC, and ABC would compete in pseudo-Olympic competitions like tug of war, dunking booths, and boat races in swimming pools. Basically, any athletic competition that allowed good-looking TV stars to bounce around on the screen in shorts and T-shirts—that was the idea.

Cosell wanted me on the show because of my work on *SNL*—especially my Sports Guy character, which, of course, had been inspired in part by Cosell's verbal cadence.

So I went out to LA for the first time and found it all very seductive. I loved being out there. I got a red Mercedes convertible and drove all around, soaking in the sun. I was like a cliché.

Cosell and I hung out the whole time and befriended each other. I remember going back to the hotel and hitting the shower one night. The phone rang.

"Hello," I said.

"Joe, it's Howard. I'm downstairs. I'm in the bar. I'm drinking vodka." He hung up the phone without saying another word. That was it.

So I went downstairs and he held court, talking about anything and everything. He was brilliant, and I still felt like a kid in a candy shop when it came to hanging out with celebrities. I never grew up thinking, *I want to be famous. I want to be a star.* So getting called to have drinks and talk with people like Cosell was heady stuff—and it happened more and more with each passing month. And soon, it began to be the case that people felt that way about *me*—even though I just wanted to be a Jersey man and an entertainer.

———

During my third season of *SNL*, I got a call asking if I wanted to be in a 1930s gangster-comedy movie called *Johnny Dangerously*, starring Michael Keaton, with Amy Heckerling as director. This was the same year that Keaton hit it big with *Mr. Mom*, and Heckerling was coming off *Fast Times at Ridgemont High*, one of the movies that defined the 1980s for the younger generation. So, of course, I said yes to the invite.

We filmed *Johnny Dangerously* during the summer—the offseason for *SNL*—so that wasn't going to be an issue. I remember how when Eddie was doing *48 Hours,* he would run into Studio 8H for *SNL* right from doing shoots for the movie. But I knew I'd take more prep than someone with Eddie's natural talents, so I committed myself to the production by renting a place in Malibu with my son, Joey, and my first wife, Nancy.

I have a great affection and respect for Michael Keaton. I knew him from the comedy clubs and from his hosting *SNL* in October 1982. Not only is he a great talent, flawless and effortless, but he's just a great guy—and hysterical to be around. Danny DeVito was in the movie too, and I had come to know him from New Jersey and considered him a friend and an incredible talent.

I was so meticulous with my preparation. I would get up early, even on Sunday mornings when we weren't filming, to practice my part. I played Danny Vermin, a quintessential 1930s film gangster—like something out of a James Cagney picture. While Joey and his mom were sleeping, I'd go into this little greenhouse attached to the place we rented, and I would stand in front of a mirror and run through my lines. I would record the other actors' lines on a little tape recorder, and I would rehearse every scene three times. So, when I stepped in front of the camera, I was prepared. It was a great experience in that regard.

We filmed in LA at the Fox lot, and I still remember our very first shot of the film. Michael and I were in a truck together—an outside shot. I had practiced my lines and felt I was prepared. But still, was I?

Michael turned to me and said, "You nervous?"

I said, "Yeah, a little bit, but I'm ready to go, man. I'm ready to go."

"Me too," he said.

And right there, Michael showing me that vulnerability and that humility—that's what he was like every day. He was the big star of the film, but he made everybody feel so comfortable.

We wound up hysterically laughing our way through the entire filming. There were a lot of times where we just couldn't get through takes because we were laughing so much together and with the other great actors. I know it was a thrill for me—even with all my neurotic, constant rehearsing.

———————

One night we went to Norman Steinberg's house. Norman wrote the scripts for both *Johnny Dangerously* and the next picture I did, *Wise Guys*. He had earned his stripes in Hollywood a decade earlier helping Mel Brooks write *Blazing Saddles*—while going through law school no less. Now I consider Norman to be one of my best friends. He has written the script for *Joey Benefit*—a movie I've got in development.

Back then, it was exhilarating to be in all this atmosphere of the movies and celebrities. Even so, I still felt more enamored with television. Or at least, I didn't know where I fit in. Everyone's automatic way of describing me was as a comedian—which I never really was. And back then it just seemed like there was more of a hard line between being a film star versus being a television star. Nowadays, it's all mashed together—online, video, movies, films—everybody does everything. Things are just different now.

I should have played the game better. I should have met every director in town while I was out there. I should have told my agents that I wanted to meet every casting director in the city. Just get me into the office to say hi and see what would come of it. Schmooze. Get my name out there.

The studio marketed the film widely, pushed it real hard with ads, interviews, and billboards on Hollywood Boulevard. But the movie didn't open as great as expected, and that's when I made a big mistake. I said something negative about how the writers had added in some material that kept more kids from seeing the film— inappropriate stuff that I still think was unnecessary. It's a judgment call, but I would have done it differently. So, when this reporter asked me about it as a possible explanation for the ticket sales, I stated my opinion. "You know, they shouldn't have put that material in," I opined.

"Joe, shut up!"—that's what I would say to my younger self if I could go back in time.

You see, I was supposed to be saying things like "How lucky I am to be part of this movie" and "Did you know we filmed on the same stage where Fred Astaire once danced in movies? I'm in awe and grateful to have been part of this." That's how you have to play the game. I just didn't understand it at the time, and movie studio executives have the memory of elephants. I learned the lesson: You just never ever go negative. Stay positive.

The film went on to be profitable, thank God, grossing $17 million on a $9 million budget. And it performed especially well in the aftermarket. Those were the years when VHS rentals were really coming into play as a way studios would make bank even if a movie had not done very well with ticket sales.

And years later Michael Keaton was told by an official in the Vatican, "We're big *Johnny Dangerously* fans."

So, there's that.

Live Entertainment & HBO Shows

For nearly five decades now, I've done live shows: comedy, sketches, impersonations, music, singing, physical comedy—the whole thing. When I think back on all the shows and benefit concerts and emcee gigs I've done—now into the thousands—I go back in my mind to how Chris Albrecht always told me, "Don't throw away your live show, Joe. You'll always use your live show."

Chris was right.

It was at the intersection of the live show material and pre-recorded sketches that Chris and I developed what became a series of three Joe Piscopo HBO specials (1984, 1987, and 1990). And it was in doing these shows that I got my first real understanding of how the business side of entertainment could both give and take away your earnings faster than I could have believed.

For my first HBO special, Chris got me $800,000. I thought, *Eight hundred grand for doing one show! Wow! What am I going to do with all the money?* I mean, I knew that I had to shoot the whole thing with that money, but there was no way I was going to rack up $800,000 in costs for one show. So the remainder would be my profit, right?

Wrong. I tell the management group about the offer and they're like, "Fantastic, Joe. Now remember, we get 20 percent of that for being your agent."

It got worse.

"Oh, and we will produce the show, and we take 20 percent for production."

Bang. Just like that I'm down 40 percent, and there was nothing I could do about it. This is the way the contracts worked

I said to myself, *This business is freaking nuts.*

After costs, I was taking home about 25 cents on the dollar of that $800,000.

With the possibility of cancer one day returning, my short-term thinking kicked into high gear. I told myself, *I don't want to live like this.*

Because of the way this went down, I switched horses and went with a different talent agency. And I developed the wrong attitude.

There was my mistake, right there.

You know what you're supposed to do in Hollywood? You take it. You say, "OK, sure. No problem." Shut your mouth, play the game.

And I never did. I fought it. And they thought, *Piscopo, he's difficult. Look at this.*

I said, "I'm not being difficult. But why should I give all that money away?" It was small-minded of me. I should have thought of the bigger picture. Sure, they're going to steal from you. Let them steal. It'll come back around.

I made the HBO special just the way I wanted to, and we won two CableACE Awards, the cable TV equivalent back then of an Emmy. I won for performance, and my director, Jay Dubin, won for production.

Altogether, I did three HBO specials and one *Joe Piscopo New Jersey Special* for ABC in 1986 (that one involved Danny DeVito and Eddie Murphy). I used a lot of the material for live shows that I was doing across the country too.

Speaking of live shows, in 1985 I took to the stage alongside Chevy Chase as we helped emcee the US leg of the one-day Live Aid concert spectacular. This event, which took place in London and Philadelphia, involved dozens of the hottest singers and bands raising millions for hunger relief in Africa. Queen's performance in London has been described as one of the best performances of all time. Rock historians say U2's set that day was what launched them into international rock-star fame. All told, Live Aid wound up being one of the signature events of the 1980s, and I feel blessed to have played a part.

Wise Guys, *Dead Heat*, and *Sidekicks*

When I saw the script for *Wise Guys,* another gangster-comedy movie, and heard that Danny DeVito was starring in it, I said, "Yeah, let's do it for sure." Danny had hosted *SNL* twice during my time on the show, in 1982 and 1983, and we had hit it off real well.

I played a Jewish guy to DeVito's Italian character, and we were both bumbling mobsters. Brian De Palma was directing—right before his blockbuster *The Untouchables.*

Filming a movie is grunt work—inch-by-inch grunt work. Eddie always likened it to a big, slow machine. You're just a cog in the wheel that has to keep going.

We shot all of it in Jersey City at the Meadowlands and in Atlantic City. It was the dead cold of winter, and the scenery was oil refineries and cemeteries. It just doesn't get better than that. For a Jersey boy, it was nice being around what I grew up with.

I remember how the Italians in the Ironbound section of Newark would bring us out homemade cookies while we were filming. Or they'd leave pizza for us in our trailers. They were proud we had picked their neighborhoods for the movie and wanted to show us gratitude.

If as an actor your films mostly earn a nice payday for studios, then you get more grace to not have every movie succeed. But the opposite is also true. The movie earned $8 million on a budget of $13 million, so the studios took a loss. And when that happens early in an actor's career—he or she had better not make any mistakes or get on the wrong side of studio politics.

My next film, *Dead Heat* (1988), was a cross between a buddy-cop caper (Treat Williams and I played detectives) and a zombie movie. I'm told it has become a cult classic of sorts, but it wasn't received well ($3 million at the box office) or reviewed well.

Treat died tragically in 2023 in a motorcycle accident while I was writing this book, but I'll always remember the fun we had working on this film with all its over-the-top special effects and costuming. Mark Goldblatt, who had edited some of the biggest blockbusters of the 1980s (*Terminator, Rambo,* and *RoboCop*), directed the movie. The great Vincent Price even played an important role in the movie; he did only three more films before his death in 1993.

In 1992, moviegoers got to see me do what few men have done and lived to talk about: I challenged Chuck Norris in hand-to-hand martial arts combat.

Norman Brokaw, my good friend and legendary talent agent from William Morris, called me and said, "How would you like to fight Chuck Norris in a movie?"

I said, "They're going to pay me for this?" Sure, I'd go in.

In *Sidekicks*, I played a funny bad guy, but the joy of the movie was getting to work with Chuck Norris. I had to train for weeks on end for the karate tournament fight scene. I still can't believe I got to fight Chuck on film.

It turned out spectacular, and moviegoers thought the movie was fun. It was a privilege and an honor being beaten up by the bearded one. It was a flipping good time. Literally, Mr. Norris hit me so hard I flipped head over feet like a circus acrobat.

I had never trained so hard in my life, but my respect for Chuck motivated me. He's a great guy and a great athlete. And, as silly as my character was, we took the fight scenes seriously.

And even though I signed a contract saying I wouldn't tell—yes, there is a third fist in his beard.

————

Here's the deal with doing movies—especially as an alum of *SNL*: The pressure is on. Your movies had better earn profits and work out because there isn't much leeway for losing money.

Comedian and actor Kevin Hart once said, "Hollywood has a way of making everything seem like an overnight success." His point being that Hollywood success may seem instant, but it's actually anything but that.

By the mid-1990s, my career had gone cold when it came to being able to land good roles in big movie projects. I've acted in another dozen small-budget films since then, but by the end of the decade I was becoming a dad again, so even if my phone had been ringing with offers for major movie roles, my personal life and family commitments couldn't have sustained that type of work.

Almost Theres

There have been several "almost there" opportunities for me in both
TV and movies—projects that might have come to pass but instead got
passed over. Sometimes I want to call this book by that name—*Almost
There*—because I *almost* got to launch or land these projects, but then
for some reason they fell apart. Because of my faith, I feel it was part of
the grand design from God—though having big almost theres will play
with your mind if you get to thinking about what might have been.

For example, I read the 1980 autobiography *Catch Me If You
Can* by Frank Abagnale, telling his life story of being a con man
and playing all these different characters. I took the concept to my
agent, who had become a major Hollywood mover and shaker by
that point.

"Chris, make this movie with me," I said. "I could do this—with
all these characters. This is made for me."

Chris tried but he just couldn't sell the concept to the
movie companies.

He fought for me, but I had gotten bad-mouthed by the management company I had left behind. "Don't work with Piscopo. He's
difficult," became the line used against me.

Years later, of course, Steven Spielberg directed Leonard DiCaprio as Abagnale and their version of *Catch Me If You Can* earned $350
million worldwide.

So I was right about the appeal of Abagnale's story—even if
nobody thought I was the right guy to play the part.

———

Another near miss after *SNL* involved me working with Ron Howard.

Ron had hosted for us on *SNL* in 1982, and after I left the show,
his people called me to say, "Ron wants to meet you at the Russian
Tea Room."

We met and he told me, "Joe, we want to do a sitcom with you. Me and Brian Grazer of Imagine Entertainment."

In my heart, I felt I didn't want to do a sitcom. But I've always been a big fan of Ron. I said, "Sure. You're Ron Howard. Whatever you want to do."

So we pushed forward. I had top agents and everything, and we were working the process.

But then I got word back from the agents: "Oh, well, not enough interest from the networks."

At the time I still had one of the highest "Q ratings" from my success on *Saturday Night Live*. Your Q Rating is a metric used to gauge an actor's likability on the screen. So with my high Q rating and Ron's interest, how could it be that networks didn't want me involved with this potential sitcom project?

Here's my guess. I think that because of my attitude and falling out with my former management team, someone might have told Ron, "No, don't go with Piscopo. Move on."

And for what it's worth, I remember thinking, *Who cares?* I didn't worry about it. I was alive, still cancer-free, and had a beautiful girlfriend.

I told myself, *Life's not going to get better than this. So take a deep breath and just dig it.*

———

Years before George Clooney did *Ocean's Eleven*, I met with Sammy Davis Jr., whom I had become good friends with.

"Sammy, I want to remake *Ocean's Eleven*. I want to put a bunch of characters in it."

I wrote the whole treatment, and Sammy goes, "I'm in, Joe." And he says, "And I speak for Frank too."

How cool is that?

So now I'm thinking, *Let's get this sold. Let's get some buy-in.* But I couldn't get it going.

Then another group picks up the idea, and it takes off for them. There's no stopping them with George Clooney in the lead role. And nobody could've done it better than Clooney. If you're a film studio executive, it's a no-brainer for you to take that package. You have to go with it.

Meanwhile, I'm continuing to wonder when my near misses will instead be home runs.

————

One day in 1985 Jerry Lewis tells me, "I want you and I to do a *Nutty Professor* movie together—with you as me. A remake."

"Seriously?" I respond. "This is great."

"You want to do this?" he asks me. "You playing me in a remake?"

"Yes, absolutely Jerry. I was made for this."

He goes, "Joe, I'll direct this. You'll love me directing you. It'll be a wonderful project."

So we go to Warner Brothers with it, and they make it priority one: Jerry Lewis and Joe Piscopo, *Nutty Professor*. But then they go and decide Jerry can't direct this. They wanted to get a younger director for the film. Typical Hollywood.

I'm caught in the middle. I tell them, "Guys, it's Jerry freaking Lewis. Just make the freaking film."

Then I talk to Jerry. And I make the mistake of being too honest. I say, "Jerry, it's Warner Brothers that's making this a priority project. This is a number one project for them. It's really something. Maybe we should consider it."

Jerry responds, "Joe, someone's lying to me."

So the whole thing falls apart, and then Jerry and I have a falling out for a while over the whole situation.

But we reconciled and became best friends. He loved my son Joey, and they became friends too.

Nowadays I'm working on the life story of Jerry Lewis, with the support of the Lewis family. Contracts have been signed with major movie companies, so hopefully we'll get to do it, because I'd like to pay homage to him as one of the greatest entertainers of the twentieth century.

Later, of course, Eddie did his remake of *The Nutty Professor* and made it work. Jerry even served as executive producer. I loved Eddie's take on the Nutty Professor, but I deeply regret that Jerry and I couldn't pull it off ourselves.

――――――

Early on in my post-*SNL* days, I got offered to do a film with Tom Hanks, *The Man with One Red Shoe*, which released in 1985 to disappointing box office receipts. This was before Hanks broke out into superstar status, though *Splash*, directed by Ron Howard, had been a surprise hit in 1984.

When I turned it down, Jim Belushi took the part instead, concurrent with his time as a cast member on *SNL*. Jim is a good friend and went on to star in many movies and find great success as the lead star in the sitcom *According to Jim*.

Looking back now, I should have done that film to add to my experience working in movies and to learn from Howard and Hanks.

――――――

As I was finishing *SNL*, one night my agents called me: "Hey, it's almost summertime. Concert season. Guess what? We've got an offer for you to open for Lionel Richie."

Richie was huge. Easily one of the biggest musical acts of the 1980s.

Hello! Was it me they were looking for? I should have been dancing on the ceiling, all night long. Truly.

Instead, I took a rain check. What? There's no crying in baseball and there are no rain checks given for big opportunities.

"Open for him?" I asked.

"Yeah, you're going to do a multicity tour. You could make half a million dollars."

"You know, I'm going down to the shore with my kid."

Listen to me. I'm whining like I'm the Doug Whiner character. Are you kidding me? I should have said, "Got it. Give me the dates. Let's do it."

In hindsight, I can see all the mistakes I made—career-defining blunders.

Of course, I always try to think how fortunate I am by the grace of God, and I see the journey that God has laid out.

There have been many mistakes I've made that shot holes in my career—silly decisions I can't take back. Actions I took that in hindsight stopped my movement.

I've seen a lot of people come through the business who I feel just aren't that talented, if I may say that. But they play the game well and are starring in films. You see that, and you think that's the secret—playing the system like a fiddle.

On the other hand, you watch raw talent like Eddie Murphy. He couldn't care less about anybody. He didn't kiss butt, because when you're that brilliant you can do anything you want.

I can look back and see a lot of things I should have done differently. I should have stayed with one management group and not switched and gone with the other. I should have played the Hollywood game more and been humbler.

But truth is, I think that when I got diagnosed with cancer and never thought I'd live to thirty-five, it changed my whole outlook, and I never came back from that. I said, "Hey, I'm dying. Who gives a hoot? I'm doing what I want to do." Once I developed short-term thinking for my career, I never went back.

I feel like I went all out, that I tried hard and gave it my all. But at some point, you're sitting and waiting for phone calls to come that never do. You're thinking, *OK, what's next?*

Common sense tells you, "It's time to schmooze." You have to work it.

Kiss butt? Was that what I should have done? Call a producer and beg for a role? It's not in my DNA to do that.

And again, with the potential for cancer's return, I just thought I was going to be dead by thirty-five. That my time on this planet was limited and would be tragically short.

Forget them, I thought. *I'll just do what I want. It's my life. If they don't want me, then I'm going to get on with my life.*

So that's what I did.

And that's where my career goals changed. My life changed. My marriage was over. I said, "Fine. I'm going to go with the beautiful girls in Hollywood and have some fun." Not planning ahead. Not thinking long term.

I got checked up every four months for the cancer—and the cancer never returned. Ten years later the doctors labeled me "cancer-free."

At that point, I reflected and came to understand myself better. Had I not been diagnosed, I probably would've been more concentrated on my career and on maintaining the life and the lifestyle needed for a sustained career in movies and TV and the true path for Hollywood success.

When, after a decade of not having cancer, you start thinking, *I'm going to be here awhile longer*, then you try to play catch-up, to rebuild the bridges you once burned so casually.

20

AN EVENING AT
THE WHITE HOUSE

I t's hard to imagine any part of culture being nonpartisan today—
let alone comedy. Every issue and conversation has become a zero-
sum contest in our polarized and fractured nation. I say this to my
comedy and entertainment friends on the left and right alike: Everybody needs to calm down. If it's funny, you can laugh.

I lampooned two sitting presidents on live national TV—Carter
and Reagan—plus Abraham Lincoln, Nixon, and JFK. Yet I still got
invited to a state dinner in the White House in February 1985. Think
about that. I parodied Ronald Reagan for four years and got rewarded
with a black-tie memory to last a lifetime.

I remember thinking, *What is this? I'm going to the Reagan White
House? How could this be happening, man?*

So I went down to Washington, walked in the door, and ran right
into the press.

"Hey Joe," someone shouted, "what are *you* doing here?"

"I have no idea, guys. I'm a registered Democrat."

I stood in the receiving line next to Sigourney Weaver, who was between *Ghostbusters* and *Aliens*. Also in the room that night appeared a New York real estate developer and his first wife: Donald and Ivana Trump. It was a "who's who" of wealthy and famous people, all there to help President Reagan play host to the king of Saudi Arabia. And with over fifty celebrities and international dignitaries in the room, guess who *The Washington Post* opened their story with? Jersey Guy for the win!

> When a White House aide formally introduced him to reporters at last night's state dinner, you could see Joe Piscopo, former "Saturday Night Live" comedian processing the possibilities. He laughed, he grimaced, he rolled his eyes.
>
> "There's enough material here to last you a year," he said.
>
> Example: "The king of Saudi Arabia came here to see how a real king lives, I suppose."
>
> Piscopo was one of the guests at the dinner for Saudi King Fahd. And just how did the registered Democrat get there?
>
> "No idea, but I'm not complaining. It's exciting. It's Americana. It's Ronald Reagan."[18]

I love how the reporter's staccato sentences and my "It's exciting" remarks make it sound like I'm doing my *SNL* Sports Guy character. All that's missing is my trademark final line: "Who cares?"

At dinner, they placed me at a table with journalist Chris Wallace on one side of me and National Security Advisor Robert McFarlane on the other. Trust me when I say that because of me, those two guys better understood the geopolitical landscape by the end of their meal. Across the table from me sat the current manager of the New York Yankees, a fellow Italian and a personal hero of mine: Yogi Berra.

We ate and listened to Montserrat Caballé, a world-class soprano opera singer—and yes, an Italian. She was doing her thing, belting out the "la la las" of her piece, while Yogi and I were soaking it all in and goofing off.

"Look at this, man. We're at the White House—with Italian opera too," Yogi said.

Over the years, Yogi and I would go on to appear at dozens of events together around New York and New Jersey—fundraisers for charities and Italian American celebrations. I was often the emcee, and before I'd go up to the mic, Yogi would say, "Joe, you'd better do good. Otherwise, I'm pulling you and putting in a relief pitcher." I loved that guy.

Yogi was about to head to Florida for spring training for what would have been his second full season as skipper of the Yanks. Unfortunately, George "the Boss" Steinbrenner fired him sixteen games into the regular season, creating a rift in Berra's relationship with the organization that famously lasted for fifteen years. But on that night in February, we two Italian Jersey boys had a great time together as guests of the Gipper.

After dinner, as I walked around aimlessly, I saw President Reagan standing alone by the fireplace in the East Room. I went over to him and extended my hand.

"Mr. President, Joe Piscopo. I was a cast member on *Saturday Night Live*. Just an honor to be here, sir."

As he took my hand, I felt the warmth in the handshake. You can't fake that. He was genuine and sincerely liked people. He caught me off guard with his friendly openness. And though the president had put me at ease, I didn't know what to say next.

"Nice fire you've got here, Mr. President," I said as I pointed to . . . the fire.

He smiled, realizing the inanity of my compliment, then leaned in and said with that grandfather's voice of his, "Well, Joe, you know, we've got people to do that for us."

It was a great moment for me. I got to thinking that maybe the president was completely unaware that I had spoofed him during his entire first term in office. In reality, though, I think there's a simpler answer: Reagan just had a good sense of humor. He could dish out jokes and take them too.

As I turned to walk away, there was Nancy—a foot away from my face. Glaring at me.

"Hello, Joe," the First Lady said, in almost a Seinfeldian "Hello, Newman" way.

I had a chill down my spine.

And right then, I knew why I was there that night. I understood how I had gotten there and who was in charge. To this day, I bet Frank Sinatra said to his pal, Nancy Reagan, "Get this kid Piscopo down there to the White House. Let him see Ronnie, and let's teach this kid a lesson. Let Ronnie put the charms on him."

I've done countless Reagan impressions since that day, but they've always been done with the utmost respect. I know Mr. S. would say something like that because Mrs. Reagan got me in, and it all worked out exactly like the plans laid by the Chairman of the Board.

21

MUSCLES & CRITICS

The thyroid cancer scare that started in 1981 didn't only give me a short-term attitude toward my career. It pushed me to do what no "funny guy" is supposed to do: I hit the gym and got shredded. Being an obsessive-compulsive personality, I took it to the limit and had a blast doing it. I was only trying to be healthy, but it got a little out of control. Let's be honest, though, there are worse things to be addicted to.

I loved the high I got from the physical exertion and achieving goals. Still, the beefcake muscles killed off much of the remaining career-boosting power of the *SNL* years.

In the four years after I left *SNL*, I ran so fast and collected so many wins in show business. HBO specials, lead roles in movies with A-list stars, sold-out live performances, sitcom producers calling for me, and commercials that people talked about around the water cooler: I was going everywhere. My girlfriend was Pamela Bach—before her *Baywatch* and David Hasselhoff days. Life was good, right?

So people in Hollywood told me I was crazy to go all in on the bodybuilding. They said, "You're getting too big. You'll hurt your career." But in the context of the 1980s, action movie stars were all big and buff. Why couldn't I reinvent myself as something other than a lanky, funny guy? The muscles brought me millions of dollars in endorsements and commercials from Bally Health Clubs and General Nutrition Centers. They also brought ridicule.

Besides all the career considerations, people don't understand the high that comes from a challenging workout. You set goals for yourself in the gym, and when you hit them there's a real sense of personal victory. I may have been frustrated with my Hollywood career, but my personal exercise routines gave me natural dopamine-fueled good feelings. And I earned a lot of money—more than any single thing I had ever done before—through related product endorsements.

Headwise, I felt the best I ever felt in my life. I was traveling from city to city to fulfill my endorsement obligations, and I didn't have worries or burdens. Instead of waiting for a cancer relapse to drop me, I kept feeling better and better.

People accused me of using steroids, but I never even thought about getting on the juice. Sure, without steroids there would be a limit to how big I could get. But remember, the reason I headed to the gym was for the cancer-fighting health benefits. Using steroids would be the opposite of pursuing health.

Before this, I had always worked to stay healthy. But once that cancer scare happened, I read and practiced all I could to keep it at bay. They recommended I eat green vegetables and take a lot of certain vitamins.

Like, I said, I'm not a doctor and this is not medical advice for you—but you can't convince me that it wasn't the multivitamins, amino acids, and lifting weights that kept me cancer-free.

People put you into one box and don't let you reinvent yourself or cross-pollinate your career. I went to a singing class once, early in my career, and I did my Mr. S. voice and started singing like Frank Sinatra.

The teacher said, "You can't sound like Frank Sinatra. You'll never make a living sounding like Frank Sinatra." She actually told me that.

———

I had to laugh when I read the *LA Times'* review of *Dead Heat* in 1988, because of all the negative things you might choose to write about that movie, they said this: "Piscopo might try avoiding any more constant narcissistic pectoral T-shirt displays. Is he supposed to be the Sylvester Stallone of comedy?"[19]

Speaking of Stallone, he was a big influence on me—on how to eat and how to stay shredded. He told Eddie, "Piscopo's got that skin that rips up real good."

Even though I could never match his physique, I wanted his advice on these things.

Once I asked, "Sly, what are you eating, man?"

"Fish and rice." I knew exactly what he meant. Protein and carbs.

He said, "I graze. I graze. I go in and graze. I come out after lunch, I'm all pumped up."

———

I also got to know Arnold Schwarzenegger at the gym in California. He's just genetically from another planet, of course, and I could never match that. But I had a photo shoot coming up, so I asked him for some tips. What should I do? I had in mind the thought that he could show me some new exercises or something.

Arnold goes, "Overhead light, Joe. Overhead light."

"What?" I said.

"Overhead light. It will cause shadows and make you look more ripped. When you're shaved, tanned, and under a light bulb—the harsher the light, the more ripped you're going to look."

OK. Good to know. But I still had a problem.

"Arnold, I've got no legs." Maybe there was something in the gym I could do about that.

"Light from the side, Joe. From the side. That will make your girlie legs look better."

Got it.

Later, I'm pulling out of the parking lot in my black Corvette, and I see this huge vehicle pulling up beside me. It's the first time I've ever seen a Hummer, and this is an H1—the big military vehicle.

I'm so low to the ground anyway in my Vette, but I look straight up at the driver in this beast, and it's Arnold. He's about twelve feet above me, looking down.

"Arnold, what is that?" I ask.

"Good for the Austrian Alps," he says.

Then he points to my car and says, "That's good for New Jersey."

True, true.

———

I was having a ball, but I wasn't being taken seriously anymore. I made a lot of money doing popular Miller Lite commercials and health-related product placements while having the time of my life, getting healthy and looking like a hunk. I was everywhere but going nowhere.

Tom Petty had a hit song in 1987 called "Jammin' Me" with these lyrics penned by Bob Dylan:

Take back Vanessa Redgrave

Take back Joe Piscopo

The song's point, made explicit by the video, was how TV culture and mass media seemed overwhelming—like you couldn't turn it off or make it go away. Eddie got pissed off by the lyric, though apparently Dylan and Petty just randomly pulled names from pop culture off a newspaper they had on hand—nothing personal was intended. Anyhow, if the point was that my name and face were all over the place, that was good for me and my career—right?

I was on the cover of *Muscle and Fitness* magazine twice (April 1988 and June 1990), bare-chested and with Kimberly (my girlfriend who became my second wife) alongside me in a swimsuit or bikini. My mug sold magazines and products because the average consumer knew I hadn't always been big or physically robust. So if an "average Joe" like me can get into great shape, the idea is that anyone can do it.

But truth be told, when they put me on the cover of these magazines, I had no idea at the time that they had such a huge circulation. And there were life-size cardboard cutouts of shirtless, flexing me that were placed in front of nutrition stores coast to coast. People started taking shots at me for the new image I was projecting. That whole period falls under the career title of "What Was I Thinking?"

Hollywood can turn on you quickly. Hence, the double meaning of "Jammin' Me," because my career stalled out, and I sensed that I was getting jammed up by the show business system. I went from overexposure to being unable to land the work I wanted. I was still making a lot of money with the commercials and live shows, but the TV and movie work started to dry up.

But I never got petty or bitter. It was time to move on from Hollywood. It was time to go back home to Jersey.

Part 5

WHERE HAVE YOU GONE, JOE PISCOPO?

22

LEAN ON ME

Helping Newark's Neediest

My unwillingness to contort myself to what every agent and casting director wanted from me made my days in Hollywood feel numbered. "I'm just a normal, regular, average guy in a business that doesn't cater to normal, regular, average guys," I reflected to *The New York Times* a few months before I left Hollywood and returned home. "You can be easily misunderstood."

I was living out in LA with Kimberly when the disastrous Northridge earthquake of 1994 hit. We're tough in Jersey, but this was ridiculous. The ground moves out in LA!

And I ran like a scared rabbit. We were in this penthouse. It was a little apartment, but it was the top of the building. And it shook. And then my favorite statue of Saint Joseph fell down, and he got decapitated.

I'll never forget. People were looking for flashlights. I was looking for superglue to put Joseph's head back on.

In the aftermath of the quake, I saw how the people hurt the most were the people who needed help the most every day—even without earthquakes happening. It was the Latino community that was hit the worst and the other communities where, historically speaking, the people were impoverished and lacking in resources. No one was helping them.

"We're going back to Jersey," Kimberly and I agreed. So we grabbed whatever we could find. We got into a rental house quickly in Jersey, just to get out of California and to get back home.

And that's when I found a new purpose and direction for the next twenty years of my life. I became focused on fatherhood—both for my own growing family and for fatherless kids growing up in crime-ridden Newark, Camden, and other inner cities.

I began to figure out how to put my name recognition and connections to use in a world full of people who needed help. Had my Hollywood star stayed ascendant, I may have never experienced the joy of bringing help and hope to people. My bank account would have been richer, but my life would not have been.

———————

I talked in the last chapter about how I got to know the inside of a gym and learned firsthand the psychological benefits that physical training and exercise can have on the human spirit. Looking back, it's easy for me to regret all that time invested in my physique—and, of course, the cost to my career from being a bulked-up funny guy.

But now let me tell you another chapter to the "muscle and fitness" story, because all those experiences laid the foundation for making a huge impact in the lives of kids who had nothing and were headed nowhere good.

I wanted to see firsthand some of the areas of New Jersey known for crime and impoverishment. So I went on a tour with Newark cops—a ride-along in the middle of the night. They said, "Stay in the back, Joe. Put a flak jacket on. Stay low."

LEAN ON ME 221

They took me right into the worst neighborhoods during the peak of the days of carjacking. I began to see what America was like in these areas. It was like something you'd think would exist only in a third-world country: kids on bikes selling and stealing drugs.

A call came over the radio. A guy had gotten popped three times in the head in his van. It was a brutal slaying.

This is the United States? This is Newark, New Jersey?

And here I was all worried about my stalled-out Hollywood career: What film will I do next? What work can I land? Sure, a fellow has to earn a living. But the fixation on these things seemed vain in light of what I was seeing.

That night changed me.

Next, I went to the Newark Detention Center, led by Joe Clark. He had previously been the principal at the troubled Newark high school, a story turned into the film *Lean on Me,* with Morgan Freeman playing Clark.

After his time at Paterson High School ended, Clark ran the Newark Detention Center. I began to learn about the strategies of this nonprofit with its goal of helping at-risk children.

I knew that I could have just as easily been one of these teens, because I had been a bad kid. Kicked out of school eight times. Naughty at my core. My father and my mother were there to direct me, but these kids are born into situations that they can't help.

There's this one teen in the detention center who is in handcuffs and shackles for his feet. He's wearing an orange jumpsuit.

Somehow he recognizes me and calls out, "Mr. Piscopo, how are you?"

I say hello and ask him how old he is.

"Fifteen," he says.

"What are you in here for, if you don't mind me asking."

"Homicide." He says the word *hom'cide* like we would say, "I got into a fight" or "I stole a six-pack." The way he answers my question sears my heart. Hom'cide.

I don't know what to say to close out the conversation. I choose not to ask any follow-up questions about the murder, and I stumble over my next words: "Nice to meet you. Good luck."

Like that. And I go and I talk to all the kids—who all happen to be young men of color.

I ask, "How many of you have fathers in your home?"

Not one kid raises his hand.

From that anecdotal evidence I begin to see the problem of father-lessness in the lives of these young men—boys who have already made poor decisions that will negatively impact the rest of their lives.

"You know, we're here for you, and we love you, and we want to help you," I tell them.

———

I went and talked to Ray Chambers, an extremely successful business leader and philanthropist from Newark whom I'm honored to call a mentor of mine in this area. Ray taught me how to give back to the at-risk community.

"Ray, what can I do to help here?" I asked.

"You work out, right?" he answered. "Why don't you open a gym in the existing structure that is the Boys & Girls Club?"

So, in 1994, I created Jersey Joe's Gym right there in Newark. I got the equipment donated, and we built out that facility in order to take kids off the street and give them something positive to do.

"Do the police ever come over here?" I asked.

"No, we've never seen a police officer. We don't know them."

The police station was literally ten feet away, so I went to the precinct on Broadway and invited them into the Boys & Girls Club.

I took a couple of cops over, and they worked out in the gym with the kids, and it was just great to watch. One guy was a giant, and he could bench press a ton of weight. All the kids were impressed, but more importantly, relationships began to be built. Community was being established. I knew then that this was doable.

Geraldo Rivera was shooting a show in Jersey. I asked him if I could bring in the police officers and the boys and girls.

Geraldo said, "I love it, Joe. Let's do it."

So, on national television, we brought the kids in from the Boys & Girls Club, along with the police who had been making investments of time into these kids. It was awesome and really raised awareness.

And that's when I started the Positive Impact Foundation, trying to create positive media for at-risk children. Later, I took my foundation and melded it with the Boys & Girls Club of New Jersey. I donated all the equipment that I had. So now, I'm the unofficial ambassador for the Boys & Girls Club of New Jersey.

That's the mission that God put within me.

————————

The work of giving back to our communities goes on, even as it takes different forms. Recently I have become involved in bringing attention and support to the Broadway House in Newark, a nonprofit institution providing long-term care for people with HIV/AIDS. I have emceed their fundraising gala, and I have broadcasted my radio show from their facility, interviewing their leaders. What's really neat for me, on a personal level, is that their location is right next to the building where my father went to elementary school. Talk about coming back home.

I returned to Jersey to give back to the places I call home. That's the foundation of the true strength within our communities—each person doing what he or she can to take care of their own backyard and the people who live there.

From that perspective, I believe God may have held up my career so I'd do the right things. Also, my turn toward muscles and fitness wound up being used for good as I took that experience and know-how and opened up the gym for at-risk kids.

And if I wasn't locked in with Kimberly and into raising our kids, I might have been thinking more about my career and would never have gotten involved in these things.

But you know, you may be thinking, *Joe, who is Kimberly and what kids (besides Joey) are you talking about?* So, I'd better explain all that, which brings me back around to my being a Dork Dad.

23

DORK DAD & DIVORCE II

Maybe the title of this book should be *How to Really Mess Your Personal Life Up and Still Survive.*

I've mismanaged every move in my life, I suppose because I'm an Italian from Naples—I lead from my heart and don't always wisely think through plans. I've made more mistakes than I can count or want to admit. I should have stayed married to Nancy. We had Joey—the best kid in the world, a great kid. And Nancy did my show business.

Look, I made my own journey. It's my own. And whether it was right or wrong, I did nothing illegal. But I made my own journey and have had to accept my responsibilities. I'm a serial monogamist who has four children by two ex-wives and a fifth child by a wonderful lady I was in a relationship with for almost a decade. I'm best friends with all my exes, and I absolutely love my kids, whose birth years range from 1979 to 2010.

Here's the story.

After my marriage with Nancy crumbled and we were in the process of getting a divorce, I began what became a wonderful two-year relationship with the actress Pamela Bach. I loved her greatly, but we ended up breaking up at some point, and this guy named David Hasselhoff came around and swept her off her feet. Look, if you're going to break up with a gal, you want her to move up—and Pamela certainly did with David. You know what I mean? But we're still good friends to this day.

So I was a single dad, and it was a tenuous time. Joey wasn't fond of the idea of Dad having a different lady every weekend, but what are you going to do? Then one night we were getting ice cream, and I saw Kimberly, who knew Joey because she had babysat him years earlier when she was eleven. Kimberly and I started talking and then dating. Joey loved having her around, and she became like a second mother to Joey.

I know what you're thinking because for thirty years now I've heard every sarcastic and snide remark about Kimberly and me: "Joe ran off with the babysitter."

But it *wasn't* like that. I felt like I was protecting my son by having something stable in my relationships. Instead of bouncing around from one lady to the next, Kimberly and I started dating in 1987, then got engaged for a long time, and finally got married in 1997.

Kimberly was there for Joey from the first day of our relationship, and I'll always love her for that. My love for her grew out of that. And then, after we married, Kimberly blessed me with three of the most beautiful, magnificent children: Allie (born 1999), Michael (born 2002), and Olivia (born 2004).

I wish I could say that Kimberly and I lasted forever, but we divorced in 2004. It wasn't what I wanted, but you move on.

In 2010, my third daughter, Charley, was born to my girlfriend Jessica. We never married but are friends to this day.

———————

One could never describe accurately the love a parent has for their child. It is a direct gift from God. The privilege of my life. Right there in your arms. Man, it's like nothing else. There are so many exciting and beautiful things in this world, but absolutely nothing compares to being with your children. I live my life for my children. My work, my casual time—whatever I'm doing, it's for my kids.

My daughter Alexandra (Allie) is a superstar. She was my first daughter and the first child Kimberly and I had together. I remember Allie's incredible empathy even as a four-year-old after the death of my father. This young child knew how to comfort her own father in distress. She would smile and listen patiently and quietly to songs that reminded me of Pop. And she had a look in her eyes that communicated her love to me. Allie is becoming an accomplished film editor, giving me the chance to be "proud dad" at a film festival showcasing a piece she worked on.

My son Mikey is an old soul. When he was born, my friend Chazz Palminteri looked into Mikey's eyes and said, "Oh yeah, he's been here before." And it is indeed like Michael is the reincarnation of my father.

Mikey travels with me on the road, performing onstage like the natural he is. He's an absolute prodigy with the guitar, and he's a great singer too. He just knocks everybody out with his screaming guitar solos. It's pretty wild.

Nowadays, he has become an influencer on YouTube, with a quarter million people following him and millions of views of his fun videos about music and guitars. With social media, either you go viral or you don't, and no one can figure out why. But he does it and it's brilliant. But more importantly, Mikey is a sensitive kid who desperately loves his mom and dad. I can't get enough of this kid.

Olivia is the youngest of the three children born to Kimberly and me. She is more rambunctious than the other two combined. But she's mine, and I love her heart and soul.

The thing about Olivia is that we almost lost her before we had hardly even gotten to know her because she almost died at six weeks old. We realized something was going wrong with her and took her to the doctor. He examined her and called the ambulance immediately.

Even as they rushed her to the hospital in the ambulance, they had to put an IV in her little vein. Her heart was racing, and she was a step away from death. They discovered she has Wolff-Parkinson-White Syndrome, a congenital heart defect that impacts the electrical system of the heart.

But the brilliant doctors at Morristown Memorial Hospital saved her that day and we got her back home by Christmas. That whole event really brought the kids and me together.

The doctors warned us that the heart could have another event like this in the future. Sure enough, sixteen years later she was ice skating with Michael, and the same thing happened all over again. We wound up at the same exact hospital. The same emergency room. Same wires in her. And I'm going like, *Oh man, here we go again.*

They saved her again that day, but it was obvious that she needed to get this fixed. So we went to Langone Medical Center, and Olivia had an ablation—a four-hour procedure where they go in and recircuit the heart. Unbelievable! And by the grace of God, she is vibrant. She is healthier than ever and is doing music production at college. She is just a blessing.

I'm telling you all that about Olivia because I want to remind myself of the importance of seizing every day to love your people—your family and friends. Make an impact now because you never know what comes around the corner. Even as I was writing this book, more than a dozen friends, family members, or former colleagues passed from this life—including my dear mother, who died in December 2023 at the age of ninety-nine. So, love your people while you can!

Last but not least, Charley is an absolute sweetheart. She brings her dad joy, and I love every minute I get to spend with her, especially when I'm watching her out on the basketball court. I'm the oldest dad there by far. The other parents sitting in the stands are like, "Which one is your granddaughter?" and I'm like, "No . . . daughter. She's my daughter."

I don't know how to put this except to just say it, but when I found out Jessica was pregnant, I had people tell me, "Why don't you get rid of it?" I would hear that because of my age and how I wasn't even married to Jessica. But we pushed back on that idea entirely: "This is going to be our baby. We will make this work." That's what we did, and the next year as I held her in my arms, and as she grasped my finger with her tiny hands, I remember thinking back to the criticism I took for not getting rid of "it." Charley is such a blessing. I'm always grateful to her mom.

Charley is a teenager now, and she really seems to absorb my work. Even as a young kid, when she'd join me in the radio studio, I remember her understanding the mechanics of the production, how I would have to go back on the air at a certain time and for a certain length. She's very astute and very aware of everything. She's way ahead of her years in her understanding of humanity. I'm very proud of who she already is and can't wait to see what she becomes in her own journey of life. I was there for the birth of each of my children. I remember the times they were born. I held them so close as they entered this world.

And for Joey, Allie, Mikey, Olivia, and Charley—they are each unique with their own special personality and with a special, deep, and loving relationship with their dad. I feel blessed beyond words.

Juggling

When you're a dad, our culture doesn't know if they should consider you to be a vital part of the family. You're a breadwinner—maybe even the sole earner. But work is usually outside the home and away from the family. When you're home, are you a vital and emotionally connected piece of the family unit?

As Jerry Seinfeld says, "Dad around the house is like a day-old helium balloon. Just floating somewhere between the ceiling and the floor. Should we play with it? Should we pop it? Why is it even here?" That's like a dad. We're always just there. If you need us, we're there. That's the way dads are.

After Kimberly and I divorced, in order to maintain a career to earn a living for the support of my family, I worked weekends up until Sunday night. Then, I would go pick up the kids and I'd be with them three and a half days until I'd have to hit the road again on late Wednesday.

The three of them were all in different schools and schedules at one point because of their different ages. Allie would go to the middle school, Michael would go to the elementary school, and Olivia had to go to preschool. I would get the kids up in the morning, always with a different character I'd make up for them. I must have done literally thousands of original characters to help launch them out of bed with a laugh for the day.

I made their lunches every day with a note written inside. I'd take them to school, and later, I'd bring them all home and make them dinner.

Getting up each morning and doing the snacks, the lunches, the trips back and forth to the school—I loved being a parent. Hey, I even changed diapers without a hitch. It's the new macho-man thing, and there are millions of fathers doing the same thing. We constantly get a bad rap, but that poor sentiment about dads shouldn't keep us from doing our job.

More than anything else I do, this is my purpose in life.

I always tell my sister, Carol, "You know when they say if a daughter looks into a mirror after so many years, they will see their mother? Well, when I look into a mirror, it's me who sees my mother! I think I should have been a housewife from the 1950s."

Although, I don't look great in a muumuu.

Where Have You Gone, Joe Piscopo?

When people paraphrase Simon and Garfunkel and ask me, "Where have you gone, Joe Piscopo?" it's really a pretty simple answer: For the last twenty-five years, I have dedicated myself to my kids. If you're a parent, their safety net is you. For my kids, it's me.

When you go through a divorce, the courts rule about who pays what and who gets to see the kids and when. But ultimately, that's just the start because you brought these kids into the world, so you'd better love and support them beyond your ability.

My kids, thank God, are doing good. And though I'm not perfect in any way, I know that I've dedicated so much of my time and energy to fatherhood. Because, after all, when you die, isn't that all that matters? It is to me. It really is.

When Kimberly had those three babies in the span of five years, it was idyllic for me. Though I turned fifty during those years, I was reborn again, with a new purpose, direction, and directive.

What career? I've got kids to take care of. I did a film here and there, but the season for playing the Hollywood game was gone. Off the radar. And that was fine with me. I could still be a blue-collar entertainer but not a glitzy Hollywood star.

There was no way to maintain a career at that point. So it was tough careerwise in that regard. But it was a responsibility that I cherished with each and every child.

———

On some weekend after my divorce from Kimberly, I opened for Don Rickles. At the time, my personal life consisted of four kids, two divorces, and an eye for beautiful ladies.

Once, as we were about to do our sound checks, Rickles came up to me and said, "Sit down, Joe." It wasn't even in his dressing room. It was just this little place cordoned off where Don was getting ready.

"Joe, I like you," he said. "I really do. You're a good kid. You're a smart kid. But you've got to stop messing around with the broads."

Messing around. That's the term he used.

"Look at yourself, Joe. You can get married. Look at me. It took me a long time to get married. But you keep having kids. Look at this."

I started to laugh like it was a joke—because, you know, this is Don Rickles talking to me. So this is just a roasting, right?

But it wasn't. I looked at him straight in the eye. Dead serious. Fatherly advice by Don Rickles—that's what was happening.

"It's a weakness, Joe. That's what it is. And you've got to stop it."

And he was right. It was a weakness. I would see a beautiful woman and lose my willpower. I don't gamble. I don't do drugs. I don't do anything illicit, inappropriate, or illegal. But I did have a weakness for beautiful women.

I made my own journey—and it wasn't without error. When you hit bumps in the road of life, and you stop and pray, *God, why is this happening to me?* the answer from God to you might be: "*I* didn't tell you to run off with a young girl." That's a reminder that you've got to accept responsibility for your own actions.

You can't blame anybody else when life takes an unexpected or unwanted curve away from the direction you thought you would travel. You can't get mad at anybody else. Just accept it. And like my dad always said, "Onward and forward!"

I was blessed with great parents. And I've been blessed by the lives of my five children. What more can I say?

24

THAT'S LIFE

On November 18, 1966, at the age of thirty-one and at the height of his career, Sandy Koufax of the Los Angeles Dodgers confirmed he was retiring from baseball. Due to crippling arthritis in his elbow, his Los Angeles Dodgers lost one of the best pitchers ever to play the game.

In a press conference, the future Hall of Famer explained how he risked losing his arm altogether if he continued, saying, "I don't regret one minute of the last twelve years, but I think I would regret one year that was too many."[20] Fans noted that Koufax bowed out with grace and gratitude, not grumbling. He kept his arm and is still alive today.

Frank Sinatra broke into music with the Hoboken Four in September 1935 (three months before Koufax's birth), so Mr. S. already had three decades of a highly successful career by the time his album *That's Life* was released—on November 18, 1966.

Beyond the random coincidence of the date, these men share something else: They both exemplify the theme of the song's lyrics.

You're ridin' high in April, shot down in May
But I know I'm gonna change that tune

The ups and downs and twists and turns of a career—especially a career that's in the public spotlight—can break your spirit if you don't know who you are and what you're aiming for.

The 1940s were really good to Mr. S. as "Sinatra-mania" took hold during the war years. In the early 1950s, however, he experienced a slump in his career, and his recording and film contracts got canceled. But from 1953 to 1960, he reinvented himself, released critically acclaimed albums, and won an Academy Award for his performance in *From Here to Eternity.*

By the mid-1960s, rock and roll came to dominate the musical interests of the younger generation. At the record store and on the radio, the Baby Boomers seemed to be losing interest in Greatest Generation crooners. Still, Mr. Sinatra's career was on fire with his live shows in Vegas with the Rat Pack, hit movies like *Ocean's Eleven,* and best-selling albums. But any performer was wise to ask, "Is my audience getting older? Am I making new fans—younger fans?"

All that explains why the title track, "That's Life," became a significant hit for Mr. Sinatra, reaching number five on *Billboard's* "Top 100" chart (it went number one on the adult contemporary chart). Sure, kids my age and I were obsessed with the Byrds, the Beatles, and the Beach Boys. But the success of the song "That's Life" proved Mr. Sinatra's continued relevance in the music industry, showcasing his ability to adapt to the changing musical landscape while maintaining his signature style. He reinvented himself and found continuing success.

Mr. Sinatra faced tremendous adversity and yet came back stronger each time. At various points in his career, critics said he was washed up. They wrote things as racist and derogatory and humiliating as there could be. But he didn't stop. He came back stronger and stronger.

"That's Life" is a powerful anthem of resilience and determination, themes that closely mirror the ups and downs of his own illustrious career.

And not to compare my career in entertainment with his, but the lyrics of the song reflect my own journey in show business. I mean, I can relate. His resilience has been a guiding light for me. I've always tried to hang in there, and I'm grateful for the ride.

I know what it means to have been a a puppet, a pauper, a pirate, a poet, a pawn and a king. These lyrics from "That's Life" encapsulate the diverse roles I've played in my career. From my memorable characters on *SNL* to starring roles in films like *Johnny Dangerously* and *Wise Guys*, I've experienced the full spectrum of show business. My ventures into bodybuilding, my stint on Broadway in *Grease!*, and my long and ongoing career in syndicated talk radio further illustrate my adaptability and willingness to reinvent myself.

I can relate to the line, "But I don't let it, let it get me down," because whatever I may have lacked in raw talent I feel I've made up for in resilience. And not just in my career. When I battled thyroid cancer in the early 1980s, despite this significant health challenge, I returned to the spotlight with renewed vigor, continuing to entertain audiences through various media, including my radio show *The Joe Piscopo Show*. My ability to bounce back from adversity is a testament to my enduring spirit.

My career has not been without its setbacks, and "I thought of quitting, baby"—but I have consistently demonstrated a refusal to give up. Whether it was navigating the often-harsh landscape of Hollywood or contemplating a political career, my determination has been a constant driving force. My ongoing performances and my tribute to Sinatra with my big band show highlight my passion for entertainment and my commitment to my craft. I have experienced the peaks and valleys of fame, embraced various roles, and faced personal and professional challenges head-on.

Most of all, I'm grateful for the ride.

Not Gone, but Forgotten

I live for live performances. That's my comfort zone. You could just be as nervous as you're going to be before you get onstage or behind the radio microphone, but once the show is live, you're more comfortable there than anywhere else in life.

When you do live shows and talk radio, it's not like film or television. There's no longevity. You've got to do it all over again the next day. I think the "love of live" is either a disease or it's just something that is innate in your chemical makeup as a person. It's got to be in your blood. Apparently, it's in mine, because I'm still on the road every weekend.

On most Saturday nights, I am performing around North America. From jazz festivals to casinos. It's a gas. I generally perform with a group of musicians and do a comedy and music show.

Every morning from six to ten, I host a syndicated talk radio show from a studio in New York City. And every Sunday night from six to eight, I host *Sundays with Sinatra*—also syndicated. Both of these programs are very successful.

But when some people talk about me, it's like they're channeling Bart Simpson's mournful statement about me in season four of *The Simpsons*: "I miss Joe Piscopo."

Hey buddy, I've not gone anywhere. It's not as if I am a hermit or out of the public's eye. Heck no, I'm doing some form of live entertainment or production six or seven days a week.

———

There's a story from when I was performing in *Grease!* in 1996 that I think epitomizes my life.

They wanted me to do the Vince Fontaine character on Broadway, and they sent me to Chicago to "work out" with the North American road troupe. I worked with the group out there for a week, got the character down, and had a blast. I was supposed to finish up with two shows on Saturday, then fly to New York and open on Broadway that Monday. Well, I whined to the producers that maybe it would be best if I just did the one show, a matinee, on that Saturday, just to be sure to get home in time to rest and focus on the upcoming Broadway opening. The producers let me slide and sent me home after the matinee.

Good thing they did because it just so happened there was the snowstorm of the century that Saturday night! Snow so intense that it *shut down* Broadway for a couple of days!

Shut down Broadway?

Almost.

The producers kept *Grease!* right on schedule. We would be in that Monday for the night's show.

Now mind you, the city was completely shut down. Including every single show . . . except ours. I was so impressed that each and every cast member showed up to that rehearsal. We all had to trudge through several feet of unplowed snow to get there.

Well, that night, we were the only show in town. The producers, Fran and Barry Weissler, wisely got out the word to the intense New York media that we were making history. They were telling the media, "Joe Piscopo was about to make his Broadway debut. Forget the snow, the show must go on."

It worked. We were sold out. And from that beginning, we would knock out eight shows a week. The incredibly talented cast I got to work with would get standing ovations every night.

After the show, there were throngs of people waiting for us to sign autographs.

"Joe. Joe! I'm from Nebraska, can I get a picture?"

"Joe, you were awesome."

Hey, this wasn't Shakespeare, but I'll take it!

Feeling good, I would walk in every night under the single light bulb of the stage door entrance. I always thought about how, when I got my start at the comedy clubs right up the block, I'd see these entrances and think, *Perhaps one day, I will "play" Broadway.* And now, years later, I was doing just that. The best talent in the world was on Broadway, and there I was. I felt so grateful to be doing what I was doing.

Just when I was feeling great about myself and reflecting on it all, some guy walked past me, stopped, and said, "Hey, Joe Piscopo! What are you doing now?"

You know, because I hadn't been doing anything since . . . whenever it was that this guy on the street remembered last seeing me.

I've heard that question many times over the years, as people go Simon and Garfunkel on me: "Where have you gone, Joe Piscopo?"

It's a good thing that "Jesus loves you more than you will know," because, as Rodney once told me, "Joe, you're only as good as your last show."

Celebrity Gets in the Way

I never was a comedian. I am an entertainer. And that's all I got in the business to do—to do exactly what I'm doing now. Celebrity just got in the way. I'm no big star, and I never really was, even though by the mid-1980s, I had become a very recognizable name in the pop culture lexicon of the United States. My unique-sounding last name and trademark curly hair, my HBO specials, movies, four years with *SNL*, those awesome Miller Lite commercials—and don't forget my biceps: It all adds up. I did break out and find success, though I ain't no Larry David, Jerry Seinfeld, or Eddie Murphy. Some people are just meteors. They took their God-given talent and combined it with hard work and a little bit of luck and good timing. Most entertainers don't earn that much in their entire career. As for me, I'm doing what I've always wanted to do: work.

With props to the great James Brown, I consider myself one of the hardest-working men in show business. And God gave me a wide variety of talents that serve me well in my work as an entertainer. Did I play every career card perfectly? No. Did I have endless luck and perfect timing? No. But if there's one thing I believe with all my heart, it's how fortunate I am by the grace of God. I now see the journey God had laid out, and I'm grateful.

I don't even look at levels of who's big and who's not, who made it and who didn't. The question is, *Are you working?* Because the journey is the fun part.

Even at the height of my fame and success, I'm the guy about whom movie producers in smoke-filled rooms said things like, "We can't get Tom Hanks? Crap. OK, Try Joe Piscopo." If you're not enjoying the journey because you're trying to be a big star, then you're going to be miserable.

In this entertainment business, everybody thinks they are Bruce Springsteen. The real Bruce is down to earth—a regular Jersey guy— but every wannabe Springsteen thinks they invented the three-chord love song.

That's OK. To be human is to be vain. My credo is that I treat everybody in the business like they're Elvis because they all think they're like Elvis anyway. But it's the people on the streets that I really enjoy talking to. The important thing is to actually like people—and I do. I have a genuine interest in their stories, so I talk with them. I want to know about them: "How are you doing? Tell me where you're from."

Retire the Radio?

Because I like talking to people so much, it makes sense that I do over twenty hours of live syndicated radio broadcasts every week. Plus, radio is how I got my start back in college.

All I ever wanted to do—and what I promised my mom—is that I'd keep a job and work hard. To build up a successful talk radio show and maintain that program certainly qualifies as hard work. I'm earning bread, and I'm making a difference.

Everyone I used to know in the business from those early days at The Improv are either not working, are remarkably successful, or they're dead. Well, I'm working, I'm happy, and I thank God every night for my blessings because there sure have been a lot of bumps and bruises along the way.

The daily show is on the New York City affiliate of Salem Media Group—a conservative network. We bring on Republicans, Democrats, and Independents—anyone who can help us understand the issues of the day better and to find some consensus in these polarized days. If I disagree with someone, I let them have their say and I move on. I don't want to be the one to lecture. Most of the time.

And I want to give a shout out to the Sinatra Family for *Sundays with Sinatra*. And to the *Joe Piscopo Morning Show* team who are the best on the air: Al Gattullo, Debbie DuHaime, Joe Sibilia and Stephen Parr. And finally, I give my love and affection to the the absolute best audiences in the world who listen to my programs. Old school radio—I love it!

———————

My friends ask me when I'll retire, but I remind them of two things: I've still got a lot of mouths to feed and support. But seriously, what would I do with retirement? Like Arnold Schwarzenegger said, "Retirement is for sissies."

When Bob Hope was asked about retiring, he'd respond, "And do what?" And about aging, he said, "I don't feel old. I don't feel anything until noon. Then it's time for my nap."

I get up at 4:30 a.m. to prep for talking on the air at 6:00. As for naps, they'll have to come later. There's work to do, and I'm enjoying every minute of it.

As my father used to say to us, hearkening back to his days in the military, "Onward and forward!"

Don Rickles did seventy-five shows when he was eighty-one and told *The New York Times*, "The only way I would stop is if my health goes, God forbid, or the audience isn't with me anymore. . . . Besides, I got to keep going. My manager told me he has to put his kid through college. His kid is 10 years old."[21]

That sounds about right.

Don Rickles's Legs

Speaking of Don, a memory of his legs reminds me to get on with life and "seize the day." Does anyone ever say that phrase without thinking of Robin Williams in *Dead Poets Society*? And wouldn't we all love to be able to seize a few more days with Robin or Don?

A few years before Don died, I was with him at an event. We had developed a special relationship, and he never spared to tell me something I needed to know. At the close of the evening, I went to find him to say goodbye; he was outside, getting into a limousine. But he was backing into it. His legs weren't working.

I was shocked that he couldn't walk. I don't know why the legs go first for some people, but there he was—full of life and spark but with legs that had betrayed him because of necrotizing fasciitis.

I must have been looking at Don with love and hurt and sympathy—and he caught me staring. Don looked up at me, glared for a second, and then said, in his Don Rickles way, "This is going to happen to you, Joe."

He laughed. I laughed. But you know what, he was right. Oh, maybe I won't lose my legs, but eventually, we all leave this world.

So let's try to focus on what's important, right?

And you know what isn't important, ultimately? Our careers.

It's a foolish idea that we'll somehow be immortal if we achieve greatness there.

When I'm on the road for an event and am wandering around some big hotel, I'll bump into a person I've met from somewhere who is also involved in show business.

I'll ask, "Hey, how are you doing?" And I invariably get these kinds of answers:

"I just did a sitcom with so-and-so."

Or "I've got this movie I'm working on."

Will you just relax? I'm just asking how you are doing. *You*, not your career. Your family, not your fame or your trust fund.

I'm asking about your life, and here's why. Please take this the right way, but the truth is, when we die, no one cares. Let me clarify. Your family cares. Your good friends care. But generally speaking, that's it.

Johnny Carson entertained us all for decades. He was at the top of his game. He could make or break the career of a fledgling actor or comedian with just a phone call or a hearty endorsement on his show.

Even so, when Mr. Carson died, he was in the news cycle for one weekend. One weekend of focus on CNN or FOX—his name being displayed in the crawl on the bottom of the screen—and that's it. After that, the young kids go, "Johnny Carson? Who's that?"

I mean no disrespect to Carson or the young kids—it's just the way it is. No one cares. That's the value of fame.

————

If you're like me—an average Joe—your children care about you. Hopefully your family and friends will remember you when you're gone. And that would be enough for me.

As Mr. S. sang, "That's life, and I can't deny it."

ME AND MR. TRUMP

B ack in 2016, when I was asked by the Trump campaign to do a speech for candidate Trump at the Tampa fairgrounds, I knew it would be the forever death knell, the nail in my coffin in Hollywood.

I thought it was best for the country that Hillary did not become president. I had no hate for Mrs. Clinton. Despite the alleged crimes she committed, I found her rather pleasant when I briefly met her as First Lady.

So I headed to the Tampa fairgrounds, after an earlier gig in Tampa, the plan being that I would stop by for the speech and then move on to another show in Jupiter that night.

When I arrived, there were roughly twenty thousand people waiting to hear Donald Trump speak. Before Mr. Trump arrived, while I was backstage, an announcement was made inside the arena that we would all say the Pledge of Allegiance. I stopped looking over my speech, instinctively put my hand over my heart, and started to say the Pledge.

When I looked around, I saw the Florida Highway Patrol, staff workers, and Trump campaign folks had all stop what they were doing to pledge their allegiance to Old Glory. I thought *Man, I'm in the right place.*

After the Pledge and before Mr. Trump arrived, I sneaked a peek in between the backstage curtains to the crowds. A lady caught my glimpse. When I smiled at her, her eyes got big. She was almost tearing up, and she said, "Look, Joe is with us!"

That look. That hope. That excitement. That *joy* from the people there that someone cared enough about the regular men and women of this great country.

It's ironic that it took a billionaire from New York City to tap into the heart of these decent, hardworking folks and seem to honestly understand what they stood for.

I never looked back.

There was a time when we were supposed to have candidate Trump on our AM 970 radio show, and my producer told me that Mr. Trump was no longer available because he had to do a *60 Minutes* interview.

I was about to apologize to our listening audience about Trump not being able to make it, when my producer quickly said in my headphones, "We got him. Trump is on the line."

I immediately welcomed him to the airwaves:

"Mr. Trump!"

"Joe! Call me Donald."

"Donald, I thought you were doing *60 Minutes*."

"Hey, when it's between Joe Piscopo and *60 Minutes*, I always go with Joe Piscopo," Trump said.

That's the Donald Trump I know.

I always pride myself on being a fair person and always understanding and even appreciating criticism. So, it is fair to say that I can't be objective about Donald Trump.

I've known the guy for decades, going back to when he was just "The Donald" in New York and I was "Jersey Joe."

People didn't see all the good he and Melania did behind the scenes. They didn't experience his loyalty and generosity firsthand like I did.

I remember back in the 80s and 90s, Donald Trump would send a Learjet to pick me up when he wanted me to perform at one of his casinos. How bad could the guy be? Always fFirst class.

He was always nice, always down to earth.

The telltale sign for me was what happened in Wildwood, New Jersey, during the 2024 campaign. We had a massive rally, with over one hundred thousand people. President Trump absolutely cleared the decks for me—opened up the whole thing so I could interview him. That's loyalty, man. I don't care what anyone says, that's the kind of guy Donald Trump is. He remembers his friends.

That's why I visited him at the courthouse during his trial. Yes, I wanted to protest that third world-type of political persecution, but it was also about showing respect to someone who's always been there for so many others.

A lot of people abandoned Donald Trump when things got tough. It is not my nature to do that.

By the way, in that horrid courtroom? I have NEVER seen resolve like President Trump displayed in the middle of that travesty.

Look, everyone's got their faults. People in glass houses shouldn't throw stones, you know what I mean? We've all got something in our past. But I truly believe Donald Trump loves this country and wants what's best for it.

That's why I supported him so diligently on air in 2024. I genuinely believe America needed Donald Trump back in the White House.

We're such a young country still, not even three hundred years old. When you look at history—ancient empires in places like Italy, Greece, or the Middle East that ruled for five or six hundred years before falling—you realize how fragile our republic still is. We're ripe to be taken over by forces that don't have America's best interests at heart. And look where we were when he was the president.

And look where we were in the years between his presidencies.

I worry that a lot of people don't see that danger. Many are, unfortunately, to quote Lenin, "useful idiots," manipulated by America's adversaries—Russia, China, Iran, and yes, even some members of the "press."

These countries play the long game. They know how to slowly erode a society from within. I saw it happening under President Biden, and I was terrified we were going to lose the country we love.

That's why Donald Trump's victory in 2024 was so crucial. He understands the threats we face, both foreign and domestic. He has the strength to stand up to our enemies, and he has the vision to get America back on track. I truly believe his reelection saved this country.

I have the utmost respect and reverence for a true fighter who defied all odds and came out a winner. President Trump has kept us out of wars, gave us our best economy ever, and has committed to help create a kind of Presidential Inner-city Task Force! (A long-time passion for me . . .)

So, with no hate in my heart for anyone and with a true love of country, I say, Godspeed Mr. President, and God Bless America.

ENDNOTES

1. "Who Is Credited With Inventing The Telephone?" Science Reference Section, Library of Congress, published February 22, 2022, https://www.loc.gov/everyday-mysteries/technology/item/who-is-credited-with-inventing-the-telephone/.

2. Alessandra Stanley, "The World: Murder Inc.; Tony Soprano Goes Home," *New York Times*, June 17, 2001, https://www.nytimes.com/2001/06/17/weekinreview/the-world-murder-inc-tony-soprano-goes-home.html.

3. Michael Immerso, *Newark's Little Italy: The Vanished First Ward* (Rutgers University Press, 1997), 1–17.

4. "Chief Hennessy Avenged; Eleven of His Italian Assassins Lynched by a Mob. An Uprising of Indignant Citizens in New-Orleans—The Prison Doors Forced and the Italian Murderers Shot Down," *New York Times*, March 15, 1891, https://www.nytimes.com/1891/03/15/archives/chief-hennessy-avenged-eleven-of-his-italian-assassins-lynched-by-a.html.

5. Meagan Flynn, "New Orleans to Apologize For Lynching Of 11 Italians In 1891, Among Worst In American History," *Washington Post*, April 1, 2019, https://www.washingtonpost.com/nation/2019/04/01/new-orleans-apologize-lynching-italians-among-worst-american-history/.

6. "Behavior: Analyzing Jewish Comics," *Time*, October 2, 1978, https://time.com/archive/6881805/behavior-analyzing-jewish-comics/.

7. Steve Martin, *Born Standing Up: A Comic's Life* (Scribner, 2008), 29.

8. Art Myers, "Funny Thing Happened," *The Record* (Hackensack, NJ), December 15, 1970, sec. A, p. 22.

9. "Honeymoon Couple Sues Bergen Motel," *The Herald-News* (Passaic-Clifton, NJ), December 15, 1970, p. 13.

10. Marc Maron, host, *WTF with Marc Maron*, podcast, episode 1129, "Jerry Seinfeld," June 8, 2020, https://www.wtfpod.com/podcast/episode-1129-jerry-seinfeld. See also Fred Topel, "Jerry Seinfeld Used to Swear in His Standup Comedy: The Brilliant Reason He Stopped," Showbiz Cheat Sheet, June 10, 2020, https://www.cheatsheet.com/entertainment/jerry-seinfeld-used-to-swear-in-his-standup-comedy-brilliant-reason-he-stopped.html/.

11. Don Kaplan, "Maher Gets Connected—'Politically Incorrect' Joins the Mob," *New York Post*, July 11, 2001, https://nypost.com/2001/07/11/maher-gets-connected-politically-incorrect-joins-the-mob/.

12. Jerry Seinfeld, "Something I Said?" Aish.com, December 19, 2021, https://aish.com/48937357/.

13. Tom Sullivan, "'*SNL*' Gets Transfusion," *The Herald-News* (Passaic-Clifton, NJ), October 26, 1980, p. 30.

14. James A. Miller and Tom Shales, *Live from New York: The Complete, Uncensored History of Saturday Night Live as Told by Its Stars, Writers, and Guests* (Back Bay Books; Little, Brown and Company, 2015), 200.

15. David Marchese, "Bill Maher on the Perils of Political Correctness," *New York Times*, September 30, 2019, https://www.nytimes.com/interactive/2019/09/30/magazine/bill-maher-interview.html.

16. Michael Che, "SNL Stars Reveal Their Favorite Sketches of All-Time," interviewed by Condé Nast, *GQ*, released on February 12, 2015, https://www.gq.com/video/watch/s-n-l-stars-reveal-their-favorite-sketches-of-all-time.

17. Diane Herbst and Aurelie Corinthios, "Julia Louis-Dreyfus Remembers 'Sexist' Saturday Night Live Set: 'People Were Doing Crazy Drugs,'" *People Magazine*, December 9, 2019, https://people.com/tv/julia-louis-dreyfus-recalls-sexist-saturday-night-live-set/.

18. Elizabeth Kastor and Donnie Radcliffe, "Fahd's Night: Fanfare Fit for a King," *Washington Post*, February 12, 1985.

19. Michael Wilmington, "Movie Review : Good Idea Dies Making It to Screen in 'Heat,'" *Los Angeles Times*, May 9, 1988, https://www .latimes.com/archives/la-xpm-1988-05-09-ca-1685-story.html.

20. "Koufax, Dodger Pitching Star, Retires Because of Ailing Arm," *New York Times*, November 19, 1966, https://www.nytimes.com /1966/11/19/archives/koufax-dodger-pitching-star-retires-because-of -ailing-arm-fearing-a.html

21. Peter Keepnews and Richard Severo, "Don Rickles, Comedy's Equal Opportunity Offender, Dies at 90," *New York Times*, April 6, 2017, https://www.nytimes.com/2017/04/06/arts/television/don-rickles -dead-comedian.html.